# HOW <u>WE</u> WON THE OPEN
## The Caddies' Stories

# HOW WE WON
# THE OPEN
# The Caddies' Stories

Norman Dabell

Anaya Publishers Ltd · London

First published in Great Britain in 1990
by Anaya Publishers Ltd, 49 Neal Street, London WC2H 9PJ

Editor: Vicky Davenport

Designer: Bob Hook
Picture researcher: Andrea Stern

British Library Cataloguing in Publication Data
Dabell, Norman
How we won the Open: the caddies' stories.
1. Great Britain. Golf. Competitions. British Open Golf
Championship
I. Title
796.35266

ISBN 1-85470-014-6

Typeset by Tradespools Ltd., Frome, Somerset
Colour reproduction by Dot Gradations, Chelmsford, Essex
Printed and bound in Great Britain by
Butler and Tanner Ltd., Frome and London

# CONTENTS

# Introduction

*A good caddie is more than a mere assistant. He is guide, philosopher and friend.*
HENRY LONGHURST

The general definition of the word 'caddie' is, 'A person employed on a fee basis to carry golf clubs and perform other services'. Mary, Queen of Scots — the country's first serious lady captain — was probably responsible for the word 'caddie'. When the golf-mad queen returned to Britain from France after her marriage to the Dauphin, later Francis II, her entourage included cadres of pages referred to as *cadets*, whose job it was to assist and answer the Queen's every whim. Today's caddie will probably tell you that nothing much has changed since 1560!

Gradually the word *cadets* was corrupted by the Scots to 'cady', meaning an odd-job man. And it is a Scot who is credited with using the first 'cady' on the golf course, namely the Marquis of Montrose, who played on that delightful east-coast course in the 1620s and wrote in his accounts, 'payment of four shillings to the boy who carried my clubs'. It can only be surmised that the Marquis was feeling pretty flush after a good win when he made that entry into his accounts, or the caddie was a highly favoured young man indeed, for four shillings at that time would have been over the top on the percentages that a caddie can expect from his round nowadays. In fact, as late as the 1940s a shilling a day for a young caddie was considered a good wage. Of course today there are small fortunes to be made in the caddying business. The 1990 British Open-winning caddie, for instance, can expect to earn over £2,000 (approximately $1,300) a round.

Whoever the caddie, the money will have been well earned; it is a safe bet that he or she will have had to struggle as hard as his or her player to get to the top of the tree — while carrying forty-five pounds of dead-weight on his back for four miles and four hours as well! It was a little different for Willy Park's caddie when the first British Open championship was won in 1860. In those days the caddies had to carry only half-a-dozen clubs with hickory shafts. Some of the caddies simply tucked the clubs under their arms in a bundle. There was no limit on the number of clubs then, and by the 1920s and 1930s the pros were beginning to take advantage — much to the dismay of the caddies, who often faced knee-buckling rounds hauling thirty clubs at a time. To many a caddie's relief, in the 1930s the Royal & Ancient Golf Club ruled that fourteen clubs were the maximum, and at the 1939 British Open at St Andrews many a caddie was seen burrowing into his player's bag before tee-off to check the requisite number of clubs.

But this was just one more duty for the caddie; since 1939 many more have been added to the basic requirements needed when he was a man with a bundle of hickory under his arm. Some of the things a good caddie was expected to know included a good knowledge of the game, to be able to advise the player on which club to use at any given moment; a knowledge of the course, the length of its holes, its geography from tee to green and the subtleties and borrows of those greens, as well as the way it played in all weather conditions. The caddie also had to be fastidious with his player's equipment, providing clean clubs and balls. Of course, he also had to be ready with a word or two of encouragement now and then as well.

As the game was revolutionized in the 1930s with the advent of steel-shafted clubs and rubber golf balls, so the caddies moved with the times. For a start they had to be brawnier than the old stalwarts had been. Some of the pro bags weighed nearly as much as the clubs. Today's caddie is required to haul around even more, including an extra towel, at least a dozen balls, two sets of rain gear, a couple of cans of soda, and various food stuffs. With all that, a player's bag can feel like a ton after a few bogeys! Add to that an umbrella and the bag and head covers, and you wonder how someone the size of little Fanny Sunesson manages to haul Nick Faldo's bag over the usual 7,000 yards for four hours or more.

There can be added extras too. For example, Pete Coleman had to carry a shooting-stick for Greg Norman to sit on in the 1982 Australian Open, and in Zambia a caddie I saw on my Safari Tour travels carried an extra that could have proved an even bigger life-saver than the carrots that are pulled out of the bag by Sam Torrance's caddie Malcolm Mason (the carrots are supposed to calm Sam down on the greens): the Zambian caddie was carrying President Kaunda's bag in a pro-am, and surreptitiously tucked away was a gun, just in case somebody tried to assassinate the golfing President while he decided on a four- or a five-iron.

Speaking of carrots, there is another important role the caddie performs nowadays, that of dietician. Providing the right foods to the player on the course can be almost as important as giving the correct playing advice. Most caddies today have a basic idea of what is good for their player during a round to provide slow-burning energy. Gone are the days of slipping the boss a bar of chocolate at a break; now it's a banana or an apple to supply the energy and get rid of hunger pains, or, as Ian Wright administers to Seve Ballesteros, a muesli bar.

A good caddie also has to be something of a psychologist, knowing when to cajole his player into making a better effort; calming him down when he's just three-putted or blazed a drive into the rough; or steadying him up from being over-confident or over-zealous when the adrenalin is flowing after a couple of good holes. As that doyen of golf-writers, the late Henry Longhurst said, 'A good caddie is more than a mere assistant, he is guide, philosopher and friend.' And Nick de Paul asserts that a caddie is 'a gentleman's gentleman'. On the other hand, Sandy Lyle's caddie Dave Musgrove sometimes gets the other side of the coin from the affable Scot, who occasionally brings his bagman a cup of tea in the morning before they play!

Good caddies have good temperaments. Just watch Ian Wright getting a lambasting from Seve Ballesteros and see if Ian ever answers back, or, indeed, reacts in any way other than to quietly stand and take it on the chin, metaphorically speaking of course. As Ian says, 'The caddie has to be the whipping-boy when things so wrong. He just has to set his chin and take it if "we've" used the wrong club.' Most caddies have their own way of getting one back in the long run. A quiet word here and there usually lets the player know he hasn't got off Scot-free. Sometimes, though, the urge to answer back is just too strong. For example, there was the caddie who was asked by Harry Vardon, who was having a dose of the horrors, 'What on earth should I take now?' Vardon's caddie calmly replied, 'Might I suggest the four o'clock train, sir?' And, as an example of the caddie who finally got his own back on his player, who had been throwing clubs around in a temper all day: the player said, 'I make it about 110 yards to the green; what club do you think?' To which the caddie replied, 'It's a 2-iron, sir.' 'A 2-iron! Don't be daft, man. Whatever makes you think it's a 2-iron? It's only 100 yards or so!' And, in a voice concealing his triumph, the caddie replied, 'That's the only club you have left, sir.'

So, for all their patience, there are moments when the long-suffering becomes too much, which usually signals the end of the caddie/player relationship. Henry Cotton's relationship with his caddie was severed through an argument, but, thankfully, not *his* argument. As Sir Henry related about his caddie, 'He never turned up that day at all. I must say I was rather surprised, and thought something must have happened to him . . . Something had happened to him all right. It seemed he lived at home with his widowed mother and, following a fight with her, he had picked up an axe and killed her. He was sent to prison for life. It was quite a shock, and I thought how lucky I had been never to get into a violent argument with him while he was carrying the clubs.'

Most caddies' traits are long-standing ones, talents sometimes learned at their fathers' feet, or from senior caddies at their local clubs. But there is one relatively new job the caddie has today: working out yardages from tee to green. Making up yardage charts started in America in the late 1950s, took off in the 1960s and came to Britain in the 1970s. Until then all club selection had been done — and still is by some of the old-stagers — by the 'eyeballing' method. This entailed looking at the flag in the distance and then judging the yardage in between before deciding on the club. The old pros used to test their caddies right at the start of the round by asking them, 'What do you have?', knowing full well what club it should be. If the caddie got it wrong more than twice, he was for the chop!

The yardages for each tournament are the single most important function of a caddie. True, he needs to be able to read a line on a green, or at least confirm the line into the hole, but getting the yardages right are of paramount importance. The player relies on his feel for putting, and all that bobbing up and down on the green, as if in supplication, is really only confirmation of what the player is reading as the borrow anyway. The joint reading of the greens may be the second-most important function, but having the correct yardages definitely comes first. Caddie Ian Wright landed his job with Seve Ballesteros mainly because the Spanish maestro had heard about Wright's yardage books — at the time Wright was compiling a yardage book for almost every championship course in Europe — and his unerring accuracy and detail in planning out the route from tee to green.

It is not an easy job. Working out the yardages means walking the course in advance, picking out points and landmarks, very often trees, but any kind of geographical detail, and then measuring the yards from the point to the green. This can mean up to six or seven trips backwards and forwards on the same holes. To make it slightly easier for the caddies, most championship courses now have 100-, 150- and 200-yard markers, and many use a pedometer — or the 'wheel' as they call it — to measure out. But it is still a painstaking process, and must be done well in advance of play. As you will see in the following chapters, a British Open-winning caddie will not only have his yardages at his fingertips, but will also have gone out at the crack of dawn measuring up again before each round after studying where all the pin positions are. Each round of each tournament is punctuated by caddies marching up and down from chart points, pacing out the distances to the green so they and the player know which club to use. It certainly has not made tournament play any quicker!

For the modern-day tour player, who relies on certain clubs being able to get him over certain yards, the yardage chart is indispensable. But, in the end, it is the caddie who is indispensable. Opens have been won or not won by the bag-man's performance before and during the world's oldest major championship week. That the winning of a British Open championship is a two-man team even can best be illustrated by two of the great tournament's champions of the past — two immortals who owe a little of their immortality to the men who strode beside them when they made history: when Henry Cotton won his first Open in 1934, he paid tribute to Ernest Butler of Sandwich, a caddie who was 'uncanny with his advice concerning the line of the hole'. Sir Henry had trouble with the links greens of St

Georges, and let Ernest virtually take over. When Henry went to collect the famous old claret jug, he said, 'Butler was a great help all week. He made very few mistakes and so often picked out the right line on the greens, lines which at the time I doubted, that I left the decisions to him.'

The servility of the old-style caddie may have gone forever, but Sir Henry's view on what made a good caddie in 1934, and three years later when he won at Carnoustie, is interesting because it still holds true today in the day and age of the yardage chart: 'My caddie Butler was content to jog along all day without speaking unless he was spoken to. He didn't volunteer any opinions on which clubs to use unless he was asked. In my view this is the hallmark of a good caddie.'

My favourite story about the caddie who turned an Open in his player's favour concerns the legendary Gene Sarazen and his bag-man Skip Daniels, who he always called Dan. When Sarazen went to Prince's for the 1932 Open, Daniels was well into his sixties, and had been seriously ill. When Sarazen saw him, he decided he gently had to tell Dan that he did not think he was going to be able to carry his bag. While Sarazen felt 'the biggest heel in the world', he also knew he had to give himself the best chance of winning the Open; and that, regrettably, could not be achieved with his old caddie Dan. So Sarazen took on a young caddie, who, it transpired, seemed to do all the things that even the caddies of today would not dream of doing, like pulling the clubs without consultation with Sarazen, and then, if the club did not work, telling Sarazen he had just hit a bad shot — it was not *his* club selection at fault.

Sarazen was favourite for the 1932 title, but it was clear he would not win with his new caddie. A heartbroken Daniels watched this all going on, and was moved to break the golden rule of not speaking until spoken to. He let Sarazen know he could straighten out his game for him 'before the bell rings', caddies' parlance for before the tournament-proper starts. The change in Sarazen's game was nothing short of miraculous when he teamed up again with the old boy, who, against the American's expectations, found new strengths. Daniels' advice and know-how swung the 1932 Open Sarazen's way. The American champion relied on him implicitly for club selection. After setting an Open championship tournament record 283, Sarazen said it was because he had had the sense to listen to his caddie at every tricky point through the tournament, calling Daniels' club selection 'brilliant', and his understanding of Sarazen's some-times less-than-cautious temperament uncanny. Sarazen was so sure that Daniels had been the key to his win that he asked for the old boy to be with him when he was presented with the claret jug, saying it was a 'team victory'. Unfortunately he was told that tradition would not allow it. Daniels, however, was content to spend the few short months of what remained of his life wearing Sarazen's polo-coat in the Sandwich pubs, telling everyone how 'we won the Open at Prince's'.

While the fundamentals of caddying may not have changed since Skip Daniels and Gene Sarazen strode the Prince's links, the financial aspect has: whereas a caddie in the 1930s might have earned only a pittance for sharing an Open success, the modern-day caddie earns a healthy basic wage on the European tour, and can look forward to a percentage of the winnings. Some present-day caddies, sponsored by golf equipment com-panies and able to command 'endorsement' fees, earn more than many of the players, as well as moving more and more into the limelight.

However, to illustrate my belief that nothing has really changed, while I was taking a few notes from a caddie in Mont-pellier in the south of France — he was telling me how 'we'd hit a great pitch in at the last' — I happened to notice the sign above the caddie shack. It said *cadets*.

# Tip Anderson

*Arnold Palmer — Royal Birkdale 1961, Royal Troon 1962*
*Tony Lema — St Andrews 1964*

'Mr Palmer said to me, after he won at Troon, "You're a real pal, Tip. Let's stick together." And we have since. I could have gone to America with him, but I didn't because I refuse to fly. Some people say I was a fool and could have made a fortune. Others say I was a good judge by staying home. I'll never know. If I'm going to meet America, it'll have to come and see me.'

One-time, three-handicap golfer Tip Anderson, born in 1932, is something of an institution in his hometown of St Andrews. When not doing his rare caddying stints, Tip can be found enjoying a beer and an occasional rum-chaser at the Dunvegan Hotel, overlooking those revered links that are a constant reminder of his glory years, and a spur to his memory when the young caddies ask him about the good old days.

One of the reasons for Tip's success as a caddie is that he was a very successful golfer in his own right; he was a true three-handicapper because he earned his three on some of the world's most formidable links. He was a scratch player at many courses, and could maintain that standard, as seventeen trophies, including the Fife Amateur Championship and two Army Championships, proved.

A major factor that contributed to Tip's being top man with the bag was the philosophy and teachings of his father, Tip Senior. The elder Tip, who earned his name for tipping cues in the snooker(pool)-room at the back of an Italian ice-cream shop in St Andrews, taught young Tip everything he knew. And that included the experience of caddying for some of the greats when they came to St Andrews, such as Henry Cotton and Flory Van Donck.

14

*Then there was the young Tip's seven-year stint as a clubmaker. Tip's first job on leaving school was as an apprentice at the old Tom Stewart clubmaking works at St Andrews, soon to be taken over by Spalding. His apprenticeship, however, was interrupted by two years of army service at Formby. As a keen golfer, Tip of course visited nearby Royal Birkdale, where he earned one of his two Army Championships. His knowledge of Birkdale paid off handsomely a few years later as he accompanied Arnold Palmer to Palmer's first Open win.*

*Tip gave up his job as clubmaker in 1956 because he thought caddying would pay more. His first stab at an Open Championship was at St Andrews in 1957 with Laurie Ayton, whose uncle David had been Tip's golf teacher. Although Laurie led the first day of the 1957 Open jointly with Eric Brown and Flory Van Donck, he was to finish out of the top twenty, Bobby Locke taking the last of his four Championship titles.*

*It was Tip's first smell of Open success, and it gave him an appetite for the Open Championship. There followed a few years as a 'journeyman' caddy, industrious years but without great success.*

*Between 1960 and 1970 there was no more successful caddie than Tip Anderson: three victories — one of them a spectacular triumph with Tony Lema on his beloved St Andrews links, and a second place in the centenary, also at St Andrews.*

*Arnold Palmer had already won the US Masters and the US Open, and was looking to sweep all before him by making it the hat-trick and grabbing the jewel in the crown: the centenary Open Championship at St Andrews. It was a hundred years of Open Championships since the Belt was played for at Prestwick. For Arnold Palmer it was more than just tradition and history that was driving him to win. In 1953 Ben Hogan won the Masters, the US Open and then the Open. Palmer was looking to equal that — and perhaps go on to take the US PGA Championship too, the golden grand slam. Naturally he wanted a top man to carry his bag, a man who knew St Andrews like the back of his hand — someone young and capable of clubbing him perfectly over the home of golf's fickle links, no matter what the weather. Tip was recommended for the job.*

@ @ @

I met Mr Palmer through Auchterlonie's Golf Shop. He was with Wilson Staff in those days, and they had written asking for a good caddie for the centenary Open.

Well, Arnold Palmer had already won the Masters and he was US Open Champion. I was flattered that I'd been chosen, but at the same time pretty scared. Still, I'd always tried hard to be a good golfer, and playing off three handicap I knew would stand me in good stead. I'd listened to my father when he told me how to act with the top players, and there wasn't a blade of grass I didn't know at St Andrews.

I went into the job feeling confident enough, but the wind that got up for our first day soon knocked that out of me. I met Mr Palmer outside the R & A building and I just felt it was going to be a bit of a funny day. Well, it wasn't so funny for Arnold Palmer: it must have been blowing over forty miles-per-hour, and we're playing with Roberto de Vicenzo and Max Faulkner in the afternoon.

We had a good session practising, and then to work. And what a disaster: Arnold had 48 going out and 39 coming back for an 87. I kept saying to myself, the wind must be bad for everybody; we'll be all right. We just had to be or my centenary Open was going to be short-lived indeed!

There was no consoling Arnold, though. He strode off the course, goes up to his room and says to Winnie (Mrs Palmer), 'Don't unpack, honey; we're going home.' But she says, 'You came to win the Open Championship, Arnold. You've got to do that.' Arnold then came to me and said, 'You've seen me play, Tip. What do you think?' I said, 'Well, I can't judge on one round of golf. They were extraordinary conditions, and you shouldn't attach too much importance to a score like that in those conditions.' I think this gave him a bit of heart. So he stayed and almost won the Championship. He got beaten by a shot by Kel Nagle. Wouldn't that have been something? My first tournament with Palmer, and the Open. Anyway, I was impressed all right. He didn't think he was a good putter — though since he's found out he was a good putter then — but he played wonderful golf from tee to green. We struck up a good relationship almost immediately. There was no yardage chart in those days, but I worked out very quickly that Arnold was two clubs stronger than me, so I just put myself in the same situation and added on two clubs. It was amazing how well that worked. I should say almost worked.

The Open in those days was one round Wedensday, one round Thursday and then finishing off with two rounds Friday. On the first day we got to the 17th, the Road Hole of course, which was a par-5 in those days, and he hit a great tee-shot. For his second he says, 'What club is it?' I say, 'A 6-iron', and he takes it and knocks the ball right in the middle of the green — 3 putts: 5. On Thursday at the 17th Arnold knocks it up to an identical spot and says, 'What club is it, Tip?' I say, 'A 6-iron.' He puts it into the middle of the green — 3 putts: 5. On Friday morning the conditions are the same and he hits his tee-shot on the 17th, would you believe, into exactly the same place, and says, 'What club?' I say, 'A 6-iron.' Middle of the green — 3 putts: 5.

In the afternoon we're on the Palmer charge and believe it or not he hits his tee-shot at the 17th to exactly the same spot again, and turns to me and says, 'Before you say anything, Tip, don't tell me it's a 6-iron.' I say, 'Yes, it is, sir.' But he says, 'Well, give me the 5-iron.' I say, 'You'll go on the Road, sir.' He says, 'Well, hell, I'll still get 5 from the Road, won't I?' I say, 'You may, but it's still the wrong club.' He says, 'Tip, watch this.' He tries to manufacture the shot with the 5, but it doesn't quite come off, and sure enough he goes on the Road. Then he knocks it up off the Road to about nine inches for a 4. As we're going to the 18th tee he says, 'Tip, you lost me the Championship.' I say, 'What do you mean?' He says, 'You've been giving me the wrong club all week.' But there is a twinkle in his eye. He got a magnificient 3 on the last, and lost by a shot. So I suppose if he'd been on the Road every day he'd have won the Open!

*The disappointment of losing by a stroke in the centenary Open was soon to be forgotten for Tip and Arnold Palmer, with victory at Royal Birkdale*

*just one year later in 1961. But although it was Tip's and Arnold's maid-*
*en success, it does not rate as highly with either of them as the victory at*
*Troon the following year. For Tip it was probably because he very nearly*
*did not caddie for Arnold Palmer at all. Instead it was nearly for Gary*
*Player — and Player pulled out of the Championship after the second*
*round! Tip is a firm believer in fate, and in 1961 the finger pointed in the*
*right direction for him. Like a jockey choosing one ride over another*
*before a Grand National, Tip finished up with the winner in 1961.*

🌀  🌀  🌀

I was really looking forward to the 1961 Birkdale Open, and
not just because we'd gone so close the year before, though
I was dying to get another chance to go one better this time.
No, I was looking forward to the Open because I'd been sta-
tioned at Formby for my army service and I was anticipating
meeting all my old friends from that time.

I'd said to Mr Palmer in 1960 after St Andrews that I'd
caddie for him anywhere. Just prior to Birkdale I met up
with him to play against Gary Player in a televised match at
St Andrews. We played the match and won, and just before
saying goodbye I said I'd see him at Birkdale. But to my dismay he said he'd got a local caddie for Birkdale, and that
he'd misunderstood me when I said I'd caddie for him
anywhere. Well, I'm really wanting to go to Birkdale, so I
jumps on the last train out of St Andrews.

The first person I see at Birkdale is Gary Player, and I
ask him if he's fixed up with a caddie. He says he isn't, so I
ask him if I can caddie for him. He wonders why I'm not
caddying for Arnold Palmer, so I tell him there's been a
mix-up and he takes me on. Well, wouldn't you know it but
we're playing with Arnold anyway.

When Mr Palmer arrived I didn't tell him I was caddying for Gary, and I don't know whether he'd forgotten or
what, but when Gary says to me, 'OK, Tip, let's go,' Arnold
looks at me and says, 'What are you doing, Tip?' I say,
'Well, I didn't come down here to look at the scenery. I'm
here to earn a few bucks!'

Mr Munro was Arnold's caddie, a nice man but he couldn't handle Palmer, who asked him too many questions. Gary didn't ask too much. He told me, 'I'm not like Arnold. I won't be asking you a lot.' It was easy — like taking your dog for a walk. With Arnold I was really involved. At that time I was eyeballing distances and clubbing him with my two-clubs-stronger method. He really did need clubbing all the time — over lining up his putts; well, we came to an agreement there — only when he asked me. Confusion can set in otherwise. Imagine what it's like if I say it's right lip and he's read it an inch left.

When Arnold played a shot, I felt I was playing it too. And when it works out it makes you feel good; when it doesn't you feel as bad as he does. That kind of thing was all too much for Mr Munro, though. He was a good local caddie but Mr Palmer made him nervous, and I could tell he'd sooner be with Gary Player and a quiet life. Mr Palmer wasn't happy either. Halfway round he says to Gary, 'Do you want to swap caddies?' I don't know whether it was for devilment but Gary says, 'No, I don't think so.' At the end of practice he says, 'Do you feel better with Tip?' There was a lot of discussion and in the end they decided they'd leave it up to the caddies.

The next morning at Hillside for the pre-qualifier (it was strange that someone who had finished runner-up in the 1960 Open should have to pre-qualify the next year, but they were the championship rules in those days) Mr Munro was with Gary Player and I was back with Mr Palmer. It's all fate. We went on to win the Open. Gary dropped out after the second round because of 'flu or something. It was a good break for me. You've got to have the luck as well. It was a genuine mix-up, but it worked out for me — and not for poor old Mr Munro.

I knew the course because of playing it in my army days, and I knew where the worst of the rough was, but that didn't count for much after the first day. As well as the wind, it poured with rain. It's not surprising people don't remember much about Birkdale 1961 but the awful weather. There were two other things that stood out for me, though. One was admiration for Arnold Palmer the shot-maker, and the other for Arnold Palmer the sportsman.

After the first day we were two shots behind Dai Rees and Kel Nagle, who we owed one for beating us by a shot the year before. Quite a good position to be in. The second day was foul. You could lean into the wind and it was raining like blazes. Arnold shot 31 for the front nine, when only two guys could even get under 40 strokes. The wind got up even more for the back nine, but we looked as though we might go in at least sharing the lead. Then we fell foul of the 16th. Arnold put his ball in the greenside bunker, and even though it was on a slope the wind had blown the sand over it. As he went to play his shot, the wind howled in again and the ball moved right in the middle of his backswing. I saw it and obviously so did Arnold, but nobody else could have. He didn't hesitate and straight away reported it to the referee. In that wind the incident could have gone unnoticed, but a penalty was imposed and he took a 5. That could have been crucial and costly.

As it was we finished a stroke behind Dai Rees and tied for second with Kel Nagle. After Nagle took a 75 in the third round, it was a two-horse race: Arnold and Dai. (Palmer's 69 in the third round to Rees' 71 put the American one stroke ahead.)

The greatest shot that ever won an Open Championship was played by Arnold Palmer at Birkdale in the last round — and there's a plaque to commemorate it. It all happened at the 15th, which is now Birkdale's 16th. We were two strokes ahead of Dai Rees, but at the 15th we hit trouble. You wouldn't think getting into the rough there would be such a problem if you saw it nowadays. The rough is only about six inches high, but in 1961 it was three or four feet of thick, willowy scrub. We were only about a yard from the fairway, but we had trouble finding the ball. In fact, it was one of the spectators who spotted it go in. I wanted Arnold to take a wedge, maybe even a sand-iron, and just knock it out safe. There were cross-bunkers to get past as well, and it seemed best to hit it in front of them and then take another wedge to the green. He agreed, and we went back to the ball.

Then he took a 6-iron out of the bag! I said, in utter disbelief, 'What are you doing?' He says, 'It's the wrong club, isn't it, Tip?' I says, 'You'd better believe it's the wrong club.' But he would have his way. All I could think was, stop the world; I thought he was going to blow the Championship. Instead Arnold smashes it out of that frightening rough, and not only gets it past the cross-bunkers but lands it pin high just on the edge of the green. I don't think I'd taken a breath from when he took his stance until the ball finished up on the green. Henry Cotton was walking in with us and he says, 'That's the bravest golf shot I've ever seen in my life.' I agreed. Arnold took a four and finished up beating Dai Rees by a stroke, although Dai holed a putt from 20 yards on the last for a three. I've seen Arnold play so many good shots, but given the position he was in, knowing it could win or lose the Championship, that was his best for me.

I think Troon was the greatest Arnold Palmer has ever played in his life. He was devastating. The ground was so hard, like concrete, but he played copybook stuff — rounds of 71, 69, 67, 69 to win by six shots from Kel Nagle. We got our revenge on Kel for 1960 good and proper, and no one else was in it. Brian Huggett and Phil Rogers finished joint third, and they were thirteen shots behind Arnold. His third round of 67 left them all for dead, and with 11 holes to go for the Open he was ten shots ahead of the field. You can forgive him for relaxing to a 69. To show how fantastic he was driving, he only missed one fairway out of the 72 holes, despite the strange bounces and the danger of the ball running off the straight and narrow all the time.

I remember a couple of years ago, Curtis Strange asking Arnold when he considered was the best he ever played. He straight away plumped for Troon 1962. I don't think it was just because he made it back-to-back wins, either. I feel he really was at his peak that year. A 67 in those conditions was as good as the famous Henry Cotton 65.

Arnold went out to practise with Sam Snead, Ken Venturi and Joe Carr. He looked pretty good and says, 'I like the course, Tip. It's hard and it's long and it's going to separate the men from the boys.' I think one hole in particular separated Arnold from the rest — and it wasn't the Postage Stamp. No, it was the 11th, the Railway Hole. It's a tight hole, railway line right and bushes left. Its a par-5, of course, and with the ground hard, a mighty difficult prospect.

We'd played fairly steady, and as we went to the 11th tee I automatically reached for the driver. I always carry the bag on my left shoulder so I can pull out clubs with my right hand, and I was about to pull out the driver when I hesitated and decided to see how the land lay. I don't know whether Mr Palmer read my thoughts — but it was a tight hole and there was a need for accuracy — but sure enough he opted for a 1-iron. He says, 'Tip, I'm hitting the ball so well I don't think I need the driver. I do need to stay on the fairway, though.' It was an Open-winning decision: the 11th at Troon won the Open for him. He took an eagle-3 in the first round and followed it with par, eagle, birdie . . . 3, 5, 3, 4. He didn't do very much wrong at the other holes, either, but to carve up one of the trickiest par-5s in an Open, to those figures, and with those conditions, well it showed how his game was at Troon in 1962. In fact, his total figure at the 11th was almost as much as some took for just one hole. Jack Nicklaus took a 10 there and poor old Max Faulkner chalked up a 12.

If Arnold Palmer ever had a weakness it wasn't with his long irons, and this is proof. He wasn't so good with 9-irons and wedges. For instance, I remember him back at Troon eleven years later going from bunker to bunker at the Postage Stamp like a lost man — at the same time as Gene Sarazen got a hole-in-one there. Anyway, it seemed nobody could touch him when he was ten ahead, but he was playing with Kel Nagle, and ever since 1960 Kel had been a bit like Arnold's bogy man. He dropped three shots to Kel and turns to me and says, 'It ain't all over yet, Tip.' But it was.

Arnold was delighted to win at Troon. It was definitely the highlight of his career. We celebrated — just a bottle of beer in those days — and he turns to me and says, 'You're a real pal, Tip. We'll stick together.' And we have ever since.

*Despite Arnold Palmer's memorable 1962 — when once again the golden hat-trick eluded him as it had in 1960, with Open Championship and US Masters success, and only losing the US Open in a playoff with Jack Nicklaus — he had a quiet Open in 1963. Then, in 1964 he won the Masters again and everyone expected him at St Andrews for the Open Championship. However, even though he had triumphed at Augusta earlier in the year, Palmer decided to pull out. It could have been a crushing disappointment for Tip Anderson, with the Championship staged over his home course; instead it turned into a remarkable and spectacular success.*

Mr Palmer didn't feel he was playing good enough at that time, so he told Tony Lema about me. Tony was the most relaxed sort of guy. We went down to the practice ground and had a round and that was it. I says, 'Are you going out again?' He says, 'That's enough for me.' I says, 'You can't win an Open on the Old Course at St Andrews with one practice round. Conditions could change so much.' Did he prove me wrong!

First of all, though, my words must have stuck because it started to blow a bit during the round, about 20 miles-per-hour I'd say, but Tony shot a 73, which was a fair score. Mind you, he holed an enormous putt on the last to do that. He played a diabolical second shot and he must have finished all of 20 yards from the hole, but he sank it for a 3.

Well, the player I was most afraid of was Jack Nicklaus. But the weather deteriorated and the wind increased to around 30 miles-per-hour by the time Jack was out and shot a 76, giving us a three-stroke advantage over the Bear. We didn't seem to worry too much about being a couple of strokes off the lead. Then we shot a 68 in the second round, easily the best round, but most importantly it put us nine strokes ahead of Nicklaus. I said to myself, 'That's it,' but I was wrong again.

In the third round — don't forget they played the third and fourth rounds all on one day then — we're on the 6th green and Nicklaus is on the 12th right alongside, of course (the greens at St Andrews meet where they add up to 18). By this time Nicklaus had been round the loop, the easiest part of the course, and he's somehow clawed his way back into contention. In fact, Tony's lead had evaporated. But that did something to him. From there Tony went 3, 2, 3, and for the next eight holes he was 1-over-3s.

When Tony came off the last, after holing his putt for yet another three, Jack Nicklaus was sitting on a tee-box waiting to start his last round. I saw him look over and just shake his head. Tony had had a 68 to Jack's 66, so the lead was cut to 7, and sure enough they met up again on the 6th and 12th greens. Tony had had a bad start, 2 over after 5, and Jack had brought it back to 1 again. Tony did no more than repeat his run of the morning. He went crazy round the loop! He finishes up winning by five shots. After one practice round over St Andrews! Unbelievable! I've never seen anything like that spell between the 6th and 18th. It was on a level with Arnold's 67 at Troon. To shoot birdies like that with Nicklaus breathing down your neck — twice!

Well, then out came the champagne, but not for him — for the press and for his friends. He says to me, 'Tip, I'm going to give you more money than anyone's ever given a caddie before, but just look after my clubs. The main reason Tony wanted me to keep an eagle-eye on his clubs was because he had Arnold's putter in the bag. He'd been using it for the Open. I'd had a feeling I'd seen it before, but I'd no idea they were that good friends! So when the young pros say to Arnold, 'Did you ever win at St Andrews?', he'll say, 'No, but I feel as though I did. Tony Lema borrowed my putter and my caddies. Certainly part of me won the 1964 Open.' Well, that putter's probably with Tony now. When he died in the plane crash I cried all day. When you caddie to a guy and win the Open Championship in your own town, and on your own course. . .

⊛ ⊛ ⊛

We've had some fantastic rounds of golf together, Arnold and me. As well as our Open successes, there were the World Matchplay wins in the 1960s, especially 1964.

Apart from the fantastic win at Sandwich in 1975 in the PGA Championship, when Arnold shot a 71 in a howling wind, hitting nothing much but 5-irons low and flat, the 1970s and 1980s have been quieter years — a bit easier, not so much pressure. He's fairly happy-go-lucky on the course, except when his putting goes wrong! Arnold talks to the crowd, but he doesn't have Trevino's constant chatter. No, Arnold doesn't like his concentration broken. That's the caddie's duty, to let the player keep in the right frame of mind. For instance, he has a new ball, which I've warmed up in my pockets, every third hole, and I know all his likes and dislikes. He's been a great player; we've had confidence in each other.

Arnold Palmer made the Open what it is today. He still tells the up-and-coming young pros in the US that if they can win in Britain, they can say they're great golfers. Meeting Arnold Palmer has been the greatest thing that has happened to me. I've made so many friends. The great thing about him is, when you walk into a room — and it doesn't matter if you're talking to senators or salesmen — he'll say, 'Do you know Tip Anderson?' It makes me feel I'm somebody — part of a team.

# Jacky (Bobby) Lee

*Peter Thomson — Royal Lytham & St Annes, 1958,*
*Royal Birkdale, 1965*

'We were leading the British Open at Lytham when we
played the fourth. For his second shot, Peter said, "Jacky, I
think it's a 5-iron." I said, "I think you're wrong; it's a 4."
Peter said, "Are you sure?" I said, "I think I am." As the ball
flew over the front edge, I was screaming inside, "Come
down, come down; oh, God!" It went over the green into
the crowd. My boss never said a word. He chipped on
calmly and got his par-4. At the next tee, a par-3, he turned
to me and said, "What club is it, Jacky?"'

If you happen to do a tour of the caddies' pubs in Southport, Lanca-
shire you are likely to stand shoulder-to-shoulder at the bar with
four men who have carried the bags in no less than eleven British
Open Championship victories. Amazingly, they all had lived on the
same street, and all had lived what one of these illustrious club-handlers
estimated as a 'good wedge from one another'. The foursome are Alfie
Fyles, his brother Albert, Ted Halsall, and Jacky Lee. (Jacky's name is
not Jacky at all but Bobby. He earned the name Jacky from Peter Thomson, who, on being introduced misunderstood Jacky's first name; as Lee
points out, 'If the boss wanted to call me Jacky, then Jacky it was.')

Jacky first took an interest in golf when he was about six years old:
'When I was old enough to be able to walk the mile or so to the course.'
His father Harold loved the game and so he encouraged his son to play.

We used to watch golf up at Birkdale, and I played eventually. I became a good golfer, a one-handicapper, at the mu-
nicipal course in Southport. Birkdale was the place, though.

It attracted me like a magnet when I was a youth, and soon as I could leave school I was up at the course for a caddying job. In fact I'd started caddying a long time before that, carrying golf-bags instead of delivering papers or milk for pocket-money.

When I was fourteen the big one came to Birkdale again — the British Open — and I landed a job carrying Toney Penna's bag. This was a big step for me and put me on the road to caddying top tournaments at a very young age. Toney's friend was a police superintendent who played at Birkdale. He'd seen me caddie and recommended me, it was a real break. Toney made the last day and the final two rounds, and I was on my way. I worked on the course green-keeping in the winter at Birkdale, and spent all summer caddying. It was bliss.

Money was tight, it was true. As I developed I became a big bloke and that stood me in good stead. It helped when I used to do a bit of coal-bag carrying in my spare time to earn some pin money. I needed to earn a bit of extra money when I went on the tour and so I became a professional wrestler in my spare time. I went fairground booth-fighting. I'd fight wherever there was a fairground booth near a golf tournament — and that was quite often. I'd take on all comers, especially when I was broke. The lads would say they were out of beer money, so I'd go looking for a booth. Sometimes I'd have to go off and strip off to fight straight after a caddying session, off the course, drop the bag and on to the fairground.

Caddying wasn't the same in those days. Now it really is a full-time job. You didn't have to get up at the crack of dawn to work out yardages. If you were asked which club it was, you just had to have a good reason for choosing it. I was wrong so many times it was unbelievable. You just carried the bag for three hours, and that was it.

I'd worked with Frank Stranahan and Bob Charles when he was an amateur, so I felt ready for Peter Thomson when it happened. I was down at Wentworth and I saw

Dicky Powell, the caddie-master, and he asked me who I was working for. I said, 'You give me a bag and I'll carry it.' When he suggested Peter, of course I jumped at the chance — Peter was winning absolutely everything. We started well over in Ireland at Woodbrook, and he said that was the start of a 'winning team'. So it proved. I played the whole year with Peter and we won the British Open.

🦎 🦎 🦎

*It is hardly surprising that Jacky Lee does not remember too much about the finer points of the 1958 Open at Royal Lytham and St Annes, because one horrible moment — actually quite a few seconds — has almost brought about amnesia! The moment could have cost Jacky his job — and Peter Thomson the 1958 British Open Championship. It happened in the fourth round at the 4th hole, and it involved a 4-iron. Thomson was going for his fourth British Open title.*

🦎 🦎 🦎

In 1958 I was eighteen years old, but already had British Open experience, so I wasn't completely over-awed at carrying such a great player's bag. Peter had won three times already and had been unlucky not to make it a fourth title the year before. I'd got his bag through my caddie-master friend Dicky Powell, and I wanted to make the best of it. I never dreamt it would be such a joyful experience — or such a tiring one. At the end of the 1958 Open I was a write-off — exhausted. We actually played eight rounds of the Open, and six of them with Dave Thomas, who finished runner-up. We had two qualifying rounds, four rounds of the actual Open, then 36 holes playoff. The atmosphere was fantastic at the end as it seemed to build up over the rounds.

We went to Lytham three weeks early and that paid off. Peter shot a 63 in one of the qualifying rounds at Lytham, eight under par, going out in 29 and coming back in 34. Who could forget that? It was amazing that someone who had won the British Open three times and come second once over the past four years should have to qualify, but the boss just got on with the job. We qualified easily, of course, and played the first two rounds with Dave Thomas. In fact I think we played all four tournament rounds, plus the playoff, of course, with Dave.

We had a 66 on the first day, five-under. Peter was as steady as a rock, keeping the ball on the fairway and hitting nearly every green in regulation. We finished a stroke ahead of the field, and Christy O'Connor was nearest to us. Gary Player and Henry Cotton were two strokes behind us and the boss and I decided we were among the right sort of company. I was very impressed with our position, but Peter just took it in his stride.

We were a shot over in the second round and I began to wonder whether he would be mounting a serious challenge. When we spoke I don't think it ever occurred to him that anyone else could win, even though the Argentinian Ruiz had shot a fantastic 65 for the second round. Eric Brown then went and did that in the third round, but at that stage I thought it was going to be between Peter, Christy and Dave.

I thought we might be out of it at the 4th hole in the last round. There we were, leading the British Open at Lytham. For his second shot, which I estimated was 160 yards into a strong wind, Peter said, 'Jacky, I think it's a 5-iron.' I said, 'I think you're wrong; it's a 4.' Peter said, 'Are you sure?' I said, 'I think I am.' But at that moment the confidence drained out of me. As the ball flew over the front edge, I was screaming inside, 'Come down, come down; oh God!' It went over the green and into the crowd. My boss never said a word to me. He chipped calmly on and got his par-4. At the next tee, before we played, he turned to me and said, 'What club is it, Jacky?' I knew he was all right then. It was never even mentioned afterwards and I reckon 99 percent of players at that time would have sacked me. It was imperative he had kept his head, because it wasn't his best round of all time. In fact we needed to par the last to get into a tie with Dave for the playoff.

Dave had taken a six at the 17th from nowhere. He really should have won it. Eric Brown and Christy O'Connor also needed par-4s at the last and that would have put them into a playoff with each other. Eric and Christy — and if I remember correctly, Ruiz — took sixes on the last. My boss kept his cool and got the four. He was particularly pleased because of Dave being his friend and the playoff was absolutely fantastic. The crowd gathered round us and the atmosphere was marvellous. They were true sportsmen with each other, complimenting one another on each good shot. There was only one stroke in it after the first round (Thomson 68; Thomas 69), so it wasn't cut-and-dried. But Peter pulled away a bit in the second round (Thomson 71; Thomas 74) and he won by four strokes.

I just remember then being thankful my over-clubbing hadn't proved costly and how exhausted I was. Two days on the trot carrying a big bag over thirty-six holes took its toll on me at only eighteen. I felt crucified. Peter took it all in his stride. I think he had a quiet celebration drink. I had a drink with the lads and then slept for a week — thinking about 4-irons and 5-irons!

The next year we were at Muirfield and I also did the Canada Cup with Peter the following year, 1960, and here he broke the news to me that he wanted to use his regular St Andrews caddie Wal Gillespie for the 1960 Open. He said to me, 'Jacky, I'm sure you'll understand. He normally works for me at St Andrews and I want him to do it because he'll be retiring after this year. You'll be working for me next year, but who do you fancy caddying for this year?' Well, we'd played with Kel Nagle, Peter's best pal, and our opponents in the Canada Cup in Portmarnock had been a certain Arnold Palmer and Sam Snead. It was the first time Arnold Palmer had stepped foot on the British Isles, and I was impressed.

I said to Peter, 'This Arnold Palmer seems a great golfer. I think he could win the Open.' Peter said, 'Would you like me to introduce him to you?' So we went to the locker-room of Portmarnock and Peter introduced me to the great Arnold Palmer. Peter said to Arnie, 'I've got you your man for next week's Open. Jacky would like to caddie for you. He's picked you out of the pack and thinks you can win the Open.' I was beside myself with embarrassment, but really chuffed that Peter had said, 'He does a very good job'. The trouble was that Arnold said he had had a letter from a Mr Anderson who wanted to caddie for him as well. I just hoped it would all work out in my favour, with Peter being such good friends with Arnold. I decided to take the boat from Ireland and go up to Scotland.

When I arrived at St Andrews everybody was standing around, and then Arnold comes out. Nobody knew him among the caddies except me. The Anderson that was waiting for Arnold was Tip Senior. He would be in his sixties by then. A real character, but getting a bit long in the tooth. I said to old Tip, 'That's Arnold over there,' and he made himself known to him. Well, Arnold was quite taken aback and he blurted out, 'But you're too old. I've come to win the British Open!' Tip calmed him down and told him his son, also named Tip, would caddie for him. Tip was a three-handicapper and, of course, knew St Andrews like the back of his hand. Tip senior said, 'Don't worry, I'm not carrying the bag. Tip my son will do a good job.' Tip — I think the world of Tip junior and I did the father; they helped me a lot — just didn't realize I'd come all the way over from Ireland by boat and by train up to St Andrews to carry Arnold's bag. I was so disappointed.

Anyway, I soon got over my disappointment because, lo-and-behold, Gary Player wanted a caddie. He'd won the year before, so I couldn't believe my luck. In the end none of us won, although Tip came closest with Arnold. He was second, ironically behind Peter's big friend Kel Nagle. I was seventh with Gary and Wal was ninth with Peter. Anyway, I'd already had one moment of glory with Peter when he won two years before in the 1958 British Open. I wasn't going to be greedy.

      🌐    🌐    🌐

*Peter Thomson had won the 1954 and 1956 British Opens with Cecil Timms. In between, Wallace Gillespie carried his bag to the 1956 Open victory. Jacky Lee, it seemed, had arrived in time, as an eighteen year old, to be part of Peter Thomson's British Open swansong, but seven years later, Queenslander Thomson decided he had at least one more British Open title to win in him. At nearly thirty-six years old he captured his fifth Open title, just one short of Harry Vardon's record. In pre-Tom Watson days, this made Thomson the greatest British Open champion of the era.*

      🌐    🌐    🌐

It was fantastic for us to win at Birkdale. It was something I'd dreamed of since I was a boy humping golf-bags nearly as big as me. I was so proud.

Peter Thomson was a very quiet man. Not shy. He was never that. But he was reserved, and he used to do a lot of thinking, especially on the golf course where he used to keep himself to himself. He'd sometimes talk to the spectators and very occasionally his partners, but otherwise he'd not say a lot.

For the Opens he used to go to the course a week or so in advance and play on his own. He'd play a couple of quiet rounds and then when it got hectic and everyone else wanted to be playing, he'd stay away from the course and just hit a few balls in practice. He was never a lover of practice. I don't know why, because he was a perfectionist. He just didn't seem able to put his mind fully to practising. He worked hard before a tournament and then just before starting he'd relax. I think that was his secret.

Well, before the 1965 British Open he did practise harder than usual. He came up the week before on his own but he played two rounds every day. Practise, practise, practise. He nearly drove me mad. When it started to get busy on the course he went to the practice ground and then it was pitch and putt, chipping — a lot of practice with his short game. That didn't half pay off during the Open. He had a fair amount of putting practice as well. Peter was a very average putter but he was a great judge. I rarely lined up anything with him. Apart from asking me if it might be 'right lip' or 'left edge' he just got on with it himself.

It was a tough course for the 1965 British Open. The rough had been allowed to get really high and that wasn't good news for us in the first round. It wasn't too windy, but windy enough to cause the occasional shot to go astray. Birkdale doesn't need a lot of wind to make it tough like some links courses. St Andrews, for instance, needs the wind otherwise you've got no test.

Well, in the first round we shot a 74, two over par as I remember then. Not a brilliant start. But we missed a couple of fairways and he wasn't strong enough to hit far out of that heavy rough. My boss used to go where the mower had gone, but the fairways were narrow in 1965 and he found trouble when he missed them. All he could do was chip out and hope to make par. That's how he shot a 74. A friend of mine followed us round and he was starting to panic because he'd had a bet on the boss. He said, 'Come on, Peter. I've got a few on you. You can do better than that.' Peter wasn't in the slightest bit put out, and he looked back at my friend and said, 'You shouldn't gamble if you can't afford to lose.' This didn't give the guy a lot of confidence about his bet, but I don't think the thought of losing had entered Peter's head. And at the end of the round when he was six off the lead, having taken a six at one of the par-4s, Peter wasn't worried.

The next day, would you believe, he shot a 68. Peter just made no mistakes in his second round. He birdied every par-5 and parred the rest of the holes. He wasn't strong enough to get on to the par-5s in two for eagle chances, so he just chipped and putted for birdies. All that short game practice paid off. He got into position 'A' with everyone of his second shots that day, and that's the name of the game at Birkdale. And he kept it on the fairway all day. I remember being very excited by his round but he took it all calmly, quietening me down. He had such a good temperament. I once remember he got a hole-in-one in the Agfa Gevaert tournament at the 16th. I'm stood at the tee throwing the clubs up in the air and whooping away and he just turns to me and says, 'Don't get too excited, Jacky. If I can finish three-three I can win this tournament.'

He made a birdie at the next, but just missed one at the last and lost by a shot. He was bitterly disappointed. The hole-in-one didn't mean a thing to him. At that stage he had his sights on winning the tournament. That was just how it was after that magical 68 in the second round. He had a tournament to win. We were still a couple of strokes behind Tony Lema and another Australian mate Bruce Devlin. Brian Huggett was a stroke in front of us and I remember Arnold Palmer was about, as well as Peter's big friend Kel Nagle. Christy O'Connor was a big threat, too. So the last day was going to be a test. It got quite windy in the morning but he got his head down and played to par, not speaking hardly a word, even to me. Everybody said he was the most boring golfer in the world but he was a golfing businessman. He never used to make a fuss about anything. As well as often mis-clubbing him I might forget to put in a clean towel in the bag or something like that. He'd never say a word. With some pros you could have got the sack on the spot.

The 72 might have seemed boring but it put him in charge. In the afternoon he had a 34 for the first nine and I thought it was all over bar the shouting. I think it was Christy we were playing with and he kept landing his second shots close. He was playing superbly — but the boss kept knocking it inside him and popping them in. It must have worn Christy out. For the last nine, though, the putts just wouldn't go in and I was beginning to get worried.

It was between Brian and Christy and the boss at the end. And it was down to two brilliant second shots by the boss, with a bit of confirmation on the clubs from me, where the 1965 British Open title was going. Both the last holes were par-5s of around 500 yards and a four at both would seal the championship. We both knew that. At both Peter hit cracking drives, the first one giving me no trouble over agreeing with a long iron second shot. He plonked it on and got his first four. At the last, slightly shorter if I remember, it had been a 3- or a 4-iron for the second shot and I thought back to 1958 and the fourth at Lytham, But this time the boss and I agreed on the 3-iron. He threaded it through the bunkers into the heart of the green. That knocked the stuffing out of everybody. Two putts and it was ours again. We actually won with those two shots — by two strokes from Christy and Brian.

Some years later I was at dinner with Brian Huggett and he got up and said, 'I shouldn't be talking to this man because he robbed me of the British Open. He gave Peter Thomson the right clubs at Birkdale!' Well, it was a fantastic display by the boss, and I hope I did my bit. I had a few beers to celebrate, especially with my mate who'd seen his bet come up in the end. Peter took it all quietly, of course, and it wouldn't surprise me if, when all the fuss had died down, he went back to his hotel and did a bit of painting. He used to paint after he'd finished playing. That was another way of relaxing. It really fitted his character. No, it wouldn't have surprised me if he'd been at his easel while I was painting the town red! [Thomson, in fact, went straight from the presentation to find his portable typewriter and wrote an 800-word report on the British Open for an Australian newspaper.]

(As a result of diabetes Jacky lost his sight completely in 1988, after thirty years of carrying the bags of some of golf's greatest names.)

# Willie Aitchison

*Roberto de Vicenzo — Hoylake 1967*
*Lee Trevino — Royal Birkdale, 1971, Muirfield, 1972*

'Lee Trevino has been blamed times without number for talking players off their game. It's a load of rubbish. He never talks to players when they are in the process of playing a shot . . . A lot of people have said we killed off Tony Jacklin in 1972. I'm not convinced. I think he'd reached his peak.'

Perhaps it is because six-time major-winner Lee Trevino shares a background with his caddie Willie Aitchison that the two have developed such a close relationship over the years. Trevino, raised in poverty, had a long, hard road to golf stardom, including some tough years after turning pro. Willie grew up around the tenements of Glasgow, and had an equally tough road to go down before he carried his first significant bag. The magic of the bag started for Willie when he was a small boy:

There was talk of golf when I was a wee boy, and I went with my father to the local courses. I remember my uncle caddied for James Braid. Killermont was where it all happened for me, though. Just after the War I carried a few bags there. To get somewhere for my caddying I felt I had to travel, and I left home for my first tournament in 1951 at St Andrews for the Amateur Championship. I arrived late at night so I had nowhere to go, but I met a greenkeeper who told me I could sleep in the greenkeeper's hut on the course.

For my first tournament you were paid next to nothing from the caddie-master's box, and your tips depended on how far you progressed in the tournament. We didn't get far, but I really got my teeth into caddying. I was soon back to do my next Amateur, this time at Prestwick for Bill Maxwell.

🌐 🌐 🌐

*Willie had caught the bug, and his first top professional tournament duly arrived with a trip to Turnberry for the* News of the World *PGA Matchplay Championship, caddying for the legendary Scot Eric Brown. In the 1950s Willie had watched Ben Hogan practising for the Open, and he had promised himself he was going to carry for someone like him. 'In the 1950s and 1960s I served my apprenticeship watching what the good caddies did — old Tip Anderson, Tip's dad, and Little Mac, Dai Rees' caddie. But I had to wait my turn and carry on learning.' The amateur scene was successful enough for Willie, though. He carried Michael Bonallack's bag for twelve years in all, savouring many a triumph with the most successful British amateur, who won five Amateurs, three of them in a row.*

*For his early days Willie relied on the old 'eyeballing' method of judging distance for clubs. Yardage charts came later with Lee Trevino. 'Your man would test you. He'd ask you what club it was without giving you a clue what he was thinking. You had to know what you were doing in those days'.*

*Willie was nominated by Michael Bonallack and Joe Carr to caddie for Nicklaus in the 1963 Open, but, due to a misunderstanding, never took over the bag. 'By now I wasn't afraid to walk on the tee with anybody. I'd done my apprenticeship and I knew I could do a good job.'*

*Then came Willie's first career milestone: taking Roberto de Vicenzo around Hoylake to win the 1967 Open. The Argentinian hero then recommended Willie to Lee Trevino, and thus began Willie's relationship with Supermex. Trevino taught Willie course yardages, Mexican-American humour and how they could win with a quip and a smile. They didn't win in 1970, but they put that right with a vengeance in 1971. And in 1972 Lee's remarkable shots from around the green snuffed out the British challenge of Tony Jacklin.*

*In 1974 Willie's caddying career nearly ended when he succumbed to pneumonia and asthma after taking Jerry Heard around Wentworth for the World Matchplay. It didn't take long for him to bounce back, however, and during the latter part of the 1970s and early 1980s he and Trevino put themselves in for further chances of Open glory.*

*Willie has had tears in his eyes at Trevino's performances just once, he maintains: when Lee put his ball out-of-bounds at Wentworth after fighting back to catch Nicklaus in a World Matchplay in the 1970s. And when Trevino added the only top masters title he has won — the Dunhill Masters at Woburn in 1985 — the tears he shed were tears of joy. 'When you have 36 holes in one day as we did, the bag can weigh a ton; your legs feel like lead. But when you see your name on the leaderboard, the pain is forgotten.'*

*Willie has caddied in the US, unlike some of his contemporaries, carrying for Ray Floyd, Sam Snead, Gary Player and Gay Brewer among others, but turned down the chance of working for Trevino at El Paso and taking his bag on the US Tour. 'It could have made me rich, but I don't regret it. I've got my family and there's more to life than money.'*

*Willie is not one for keeping too many records, but one thing he'll always remember is the remarkable coincidence of his three Open Championship victories. Each of the three — Robert de Vincenzo in 1967 and Lee Trevino in 1971 and 1972 — was achieved with the same score of 276. Each one was an Open milestone too. The 1967 victory was an emotion-charged event, bringing de Vicenzo the title he richly deserved after four third places and a second, and the result the public wanted. Trevino's 1971 win was in the 100th Open, although the 1960 Championship had, of course, been the centenary event. And Trevino made it a double after winning the US Open. (Actually, it was a triple because he had also just won the Canadian Open a few days before.) Then Trevino's 1972 success made it back-to-back Opens for the Mexican-American.*

*The 1970s also brought about a confrontation between two men: Trevino and Tony Jacklin. Willie Aitchison played his part, too, in the drama. Willie's story starts a few years before his first Open triumph, and bears out his theory that his golf destiny was 'written in the stars'.*

After the 1963 Walker Cup, Michael Bonallack and Joe Carr wrote a letter to Jack Nicklaus nominating me to caddie for him at Lytham. Due to business commitments, Jack never answered. I'd been caddying for Ralph Moffatt on the pro circuit and got him through the pre-qualifier at Fairhaven, so I told him I'd be caddying for him in the Open as I'd heard nothing from Jack.

When Nicklaus did finally track me down he told me the bag was still mine if I wanted it, but I told him I'd already committed myself, so I gave up the chance. I'm not saying I'd have been good for him or him for me, but it did provide a link in a chain that was to tie me to glory in the Open.

I then did a series of films with Robert de Vicenzo, big money in those days, which convinced me at the time that Roberto would win the 1967 Open. We played an exhibition match with Jack Nicklaus just before the 1967 Open and, as we say in Scotland, 'golfed the heed off him'. Roberto gave the exhibition; Nicklaus watched.

Roberto also won the Nine Nations Tournament — a charity event with players drawn from the top — prior to the Open. Again Roberto was above everyone else. There was one department, however, that he'd convinced himself he was not so good in: putting. He was incredible; he could shoot rounds of 64 and 65 any day of the week — and to do that you've got to be a reasonable putter. That was typical of Roberto, though: he had the ability but could never convince himself.

Come the tournament he certainly putted well enough, and we were there after a 70 in the first round and a shot behind Jack Nicklaus after the second round. Roberto played beautifully in the third round and we progressed to two strokes ahead of the field after he shot a 67. We led Nicklaus by those two shots and Gary Player by three. But the bookies still considered Roberto the outsider of the three. I can remember him saying, as we walked down the second fairway, 'Willie, if I can win these people [the gallery] over from Jack [Nicklaus] so that they want me to win, I'll win for them.'

Well, by the 9th we still held our two-stroke lead, and slowly but surely the galleries got bigger and bigger. As the people came flocking to see him, it was as if Roberto's back got broader and he held his head higher. His pride really started to show. It seemed nothing could stop him, but there was still that chance of losing it to be overcome, and sure enough it came. I've always been a believer in fate, and that one shot can win or lose an Open. Roberto's shot came at the 16th.

In those days Open Championship crowd-control was done with miles of wooden fencing. The crowd had now swelled to huge numbers as we stood on the 16th tee. The drive is a dog-leg around the out-of-bounds protecting the practice range. You had to drive leftish to position yourself far enough down the fairway to get a pitch into the green. As Roberto was coming down from the top of his back-swing, the spectators leaned forward on to the fencing causing a crack like thunder. You could see Roberto start as he hit into the ball. My stomach turned over as I watched the ball heading for the out-of-bounds, but to my relief it looked as though it had stayed in, even if it seemed in an awful spot. As it turned out it had landed in a position that couldn't have been more perfect for what was to happen next.

I was eyeballing distances at that time, and had no real idea how far Roberto had to clear the out-of-bounds and a wee bank that ran round the hole, but we had a strong breeze behind us going from right to left. Roberto says, 'Willie, which way do we go?' Well, I looked at the shot and saw it. I could see it sailing over the trouble and landing on the green. I said, 'There's only one way to go — right across the out-of-bounds.' I handed him the 3-wood. You just know when a shot is perfect because you hear that tell-tale crack when it comes out of the middle of the club. That's just what happened — right up to the stick. We birdied the hole and held our two-shot lead.

On the 18th tee we hit the same 3-wood, and as we walked down the fairway the crowds were massed around the last green; the noise was unbelievable. Roberto had tears running down his face before he played his second shot. He said to me, 'Willie, just put a club in my hand that's going to get me on the green. I don't care what it is, I get two putts anyway.' He hit an 8-iron to 12 feet and started walking forward. It was a great sensation. The crowd was shouting 'Viva Roberto!' and the volume grew louder and louder.

Well, Roberto had his two putts, and the crowd was slapping my back until it was black-and-blue. They were doing it for Roberto, he was such a lovable character. He didn't have any airs and graces. Straight after the Open he was offered a Rolls Royce to go out and celebrate his win. I had an old camping van that I lived in during tournaments, and he chose to go with me in it for a meal in Chinatown in Liverpool.

🌐 🌐 🌐

*The late 1960s and early 1970s saw Lee Trevino ruling the roost on both sides of the Pond. Well, almost ruling it: one player stood in his way — Tony Jacklin. Some say 1972 was a fight to the death, which left Jacklin as the slain gladiator. But before Willie was involved in these epic encounters, the no-nonsense Glaswegian had his own battle to fight for Trevino's bag.*

🌐 🌐 🌐

At 44 Roberto de Vicenzo thought his time at the top was running out, so it was a real boost for me when he spoke to Lee Trevino. I got a letter from Lee saying I'd be carrying his bag for the 1968 Alcan at Birkdale and for the World Matchplay.

I went to Southport and was waiting at the hotel for Lee when I saw him roll up. This guy gets out of his car and takes Lee's clubs out. When I asked Lee what's going on, he told me this guy had met him at the airport and that he had a letter and had said he'd caddied for Henry Cotton. I was furious, and said the guy had certainly not caddied for Cotton when he won, and that in his later years Cotton had had several caddies. I thought Lee had been taken for a ride, and said so. Lee decided that this guy would caddie one day and me the next, and he would assess for himself who would carry his bag. I had no fear of my abilities at Birkdale, so I thought, fine.

This guy went out with Lee next day, and I was standing at the back of the 9th green when Lee's manager came running up to me and said, 'Willie, you've got to take the bag — Lee's fired the other guy.' I was glad. It'd been an embarrassment to me, but I said I wasn't taking the bag, that the other guy could finish the round and that I'd wait until tomorrow. Next day the place is flooded so I don't get a chance to play with Trevino, just stand on the practice ground and watch him hit balls. But I was impressed, specially by how he could shape shots, and I said, 'This is the guy for me.'

We went out in the first round and Lee didn't ask me anything until he'd hit his drive. Then he said, 'What have you got, Willie?' I thought he was asking me what club, so I said, 'A 7-iron,' but what he wanted was the yardage. I said, 'I don't know. I've never used a yardage in my life; all I know is that it's a 7-iron to the middle of the green.' We went around 72 holes on joint agreement as to what clubs to use, and we only missed six greens.

Lee says at the end of the tournament, which he only missed winning because his putting let him down, 'Great job, well done. I didn't think it was possible for somebody to stand in the middle of the fairway and say it's an iron of any description. But you'll have to get me yardages.' I said he'd have to teach me how to do it. It was all done by pacing, no wheels. I compared my yardages with a wheel once, and we were no more than two paces out for the whole course. In fact, I became so proficient — I used to go over and over them first thing in the mornings — that I finished pulling up Trevino on a couple of occasions. One of them was at Muirfield in 1972, and I believe it turned the Open for us. Players can forget, but you'd better be 100 percent right.

And if you're putting him right over clubs, you'd better be 101 percent right if you're telling him that what he's got in mind is the wrong thing. However, no sensible caddie has a right to start pulling out clubs until their boss says so. Only if you think he's making a mistake should you say a word — then you have to have the courage of your convictions.

Everyone calls the 1970 Open the one Doug Sanders threw away, but I think we should have won it. We led by two shots going into the last round, and when it blew on the last day, I didn't think anybody could beat Trevino. He'd been dropping drives at my feet on the beach in practice. He wasn't even afraid of Nicklaus, but of Doug himself. Lee said to me, 'If I can beat Sanders, I'll win the Open. That guy can play the wind.' We 3-putted six times in the last round. We were on the greens fine, but we couldn't get off them. Give us half those 3-putts and we'd have tied.

It brings me back to the Nicklaus chain, and how a shot can swing an Open. Actually, this time it was two shots: first poor old Doug's missed putt and then the shot Nicklaus put through the green on the 18th in the playoff. If the greenkeeper had cut the rough at the back of the last, Nicklaus would have gone out-of-bounds and Sanders would have won. I think Sanders choked when he missed that short putt to win.

🐢 🐢 🐢

*Tony Jacklin had won the 1960 Open and the 1970 US Open, and his huge British following was going to make sure that he did what they'd hoped he'd do in 1970 at St Andrews, and win the 1971 Open at Birkdale. However, the partisan antics of the British gallery only served to fire up Lee Trevino. The vendetta between Trevino and Jacklin and the British gallery proved unrequited in the end. A smiling Formosan by the adopted name of Mr Lu, who had thousands of Britons — including one Willie Aitchison — wearing and raising porkpie hats, proved to be the major talking point of the 1971 Open.*

After the 1970 Open, the British crowd felt Tony Jacklin had the right to win the 1971 Open. It was generally felt he would have won at St Andrews after his 29 for the first nine in the first round if he hadn't had part of the round washed out and had to continue the next day.

Knowing how the crowd was on Tony's side and treating him as the hero only seemed to make Lee more determined. There were times in 1971 when the crowd became quite bad-mannered, for example clapping when Lee missed a putt. In the beginning Lee took it to heart, and at one time threatened to walk off the course. It made him feel he wanted to punish the crowd and fired him to say, 'If this is what they think of me and what they think of Jacklin, I'll make sure he never finishes in front of me again.' There was never any nastiness between Lee and Tony, but it fired them both up; they were both determined to beat the other. After a birdie at the first, we ran into a bit of trouble at the 6th, a hole Lee had criticized because he felt you shouldn't have to 'lay up' on any par-4 in an Open. This is to 468 yards with a ridge and bunkers on the dog-leg. We'd discussed taking a 1-iron, but he insisted on a 3-wood and, although he got a bad bounce, put it in the sand and took a bogey. His words when we met at the start of the Championship kept coming back: 'Willie, I'm going to win the Open for you this week. No one in the world can beat me. If anything beats us it will be bad luck.'

Having got over the bad luck at the 6th we went on to a 69. Jacklin had a 69 as well and we were locked together after he and Lee both had second-round 70s. We'd finished off the second round with an eagle when Lee put one in from miles away, and in the third round he seemed to be holing putts right, left and centre, which was a good job because we'd fallen foul of the 6th again, for the third time.

At the 14th, the par-5, which is now the 15th, Jacklin looked at the scoreboard and Lee says to him 'Tony, don't look at the scoreboard because I can beat all of them up there. You beat this little Mex and you'll win the Champion-

ship.' We finished up 11 under and two in front of Tony and
Mr Lu. I became very emotionally involved in the last round
because everything Lee touched went in the damned hole.
We even got the better of the 6th at last, with almost a tap-in
for birdie. Everything seemed to be plain sailing now as we
came to the 17th. We were several shots in hand of Mr Lu
and the rest of the field, but at this point Lee's words about
bad luck started to haunt me.

He never hit a bad shot off the tee; it just didn't come
back as far as he thought it would. He hit the ball left to right
and he shaped it on the left-hand side on a sand dune, but it
dropped in the dune on top of a hillock. People couldn't see
the danger we were in — in fact Lee couldn't see it either —
because it just looked as though his ball was in a sand hole.
He decided to play it like a bunker shot, nothing fancy
because we were three in the lead; he only wanted to put it
out on the fairway and make a par 5. However, unknown to
Lee, under his ball were bramble runners, so that when he
came down to it, his hand got turned and he only moved
the ball a few inches.

We were on the green for five shots, and Mr Lu was on
the side of the green for two. He should have made birdie;
he had the greatest opportunity to win the Open. Unfortunately for him he made par and we made seven to stay one
shot ahead. But Mr Lu got back into it down the last. He hit
his drive down the left close to a bunker. We were down the
middle. I remember seeing his ball disappear into what I
thought was sand dunes left, but he'd hit a woman on the
head and nearly killed her, and his ball had flown back 60 or
70 yards into the fairway. We had quite a simple shot to
make the green, and Lee says to me, 'Willie, I'm only interested in getting to the middle of the green.' I says, 'It's a
7-iron,' thinking, 'This is where we came in!', and he hits it
through the back of the green.

I turned around to see Mr Lu playing what I thought
was his third shot. I didn't know about the woman and
thought he'd chipped from the left-hand side of the fairway

to the right-hand side. He knocked it up to about six or eight feet, but, not knowing the circumstances, I wasn't worried. When it did dawn on me it was too late. I thought we had three to win, but it was two because Mr Lu got his birdie. I was almost as casual as Lee when he tapped in his short putt for the Open. I thought back to the 17th and remembered Lee's words: 'Mr Lu doesn't want to win the Open Championship.' I remembered them again when Tony Jacklin did the same thing at the very next Open — and, amazingly, at the 17th again.

A lot of people have said we killed off Tony Jacklin in 1972, but I'm not convinced it was down to Lee Trevino. So many things happened over the last two rounds, it's sometimes hard to remember the first two; I just know it was Trevino versus Jacklin again in the third round and, of course, they were playing together once more.

It had been a tight couple of rounds, but the two were a shot ahead of the field. By the 11th things were really starting to heat up. Lee and I were feeling the tension. Not that we'd actually fallen out, but I'd walked away to check the markers and I had 127 to the hole and Lee said it was 147 — and that's a difference between an eight and a seven — so I said, 'You got it wrong.' Now Trevino's eyesight is great, but his eyeballing isn't as good as mine. He says, 'You'd better be **** right.' He dug into the bag and pulled out an 8-iron. The ball finished up three feet from the stick. I got the greatest enjoyment from that.

Everyone talks about the times Lee chipped in. Two of them came in the third round. The bunker shot was the best one. Lee was on a downslope, and it seemed absolutely impossible for him to finish close. He hit the pin halfway up and it was going like a rocket — that was the shot which I think won us the Open. It started that great birdie run by Lee. Coming to the 18th, he said he'd never had five birdies in a row, and I thought perhaps it was going to stay that way because he put his second way through the green. He did no more than chip that one in as well, and it gave us the lead.

On to the last day and Nicklaus — who was putting in a charge in front of us attempting the third part of the grand slam, having won the Masters and the US Open in 1972 — and everything was going reasonably well until the 7th, the hare hole. We'd seen the hare at the 4th and it reappeared again, dashing around right in Lee's vision as he was putting, which cost him a stroke. Lee kept on the attack despite this and the fact that Nicklaus was on a roll. At the 9th tee Lee insisted on playing his driver because the Bear was on the run. He had been using the 1-iron, even though it was a par-5, but he was afraid of dropping behind. I didn't want him to hit the driver because accuracy was the key to this hole, and I said, 'You're not going to have it.' He says, 'Yes, I am.' It was a real yo-yo on the tee. Well, I'm there to carry out orders, so I relented. He landed in the rough! As it happened it wasn't a bad lie, so instead of 1-iron, 2-iron to the green, he's now playing driver, 5-iron. He made the eagle, got in front of Nicklaus, and turns and says, 'He'll never get past me now.'

Perhaps it was something to do with our difference of opinion on the tee, I don't know — but all through this championship Lee had never asked me to read a putt for him. He did on the 9th green in the last round. It was a 15- to 20-footer, and luckily for me it went in. He has never asked me to read many putts; he's such a good reader of greens, and he says a professional golfer should putt by feel. He doesn't need me for that.

By the 17th we knew what we had to do. Nicklaus had finished, so if Jacklin and Trevino parred the last two holes, they'd have a playoff. They both knew that as we walked off the 16th. Lots of people don't know what happened next. Trevino is all teed-up and in the process of taking his club back when a guy comes out of the crowd in front of him with a camera on his shoulder and walks right across the fairway. Lee stops, walks away from his ball and regroups. He takes a practice swing, sets himself again, looks at the target — and what happens? This cameraman's pal wanders out with a tripod, and also walks straight across the fairway. Rather than wait for a third guy, Lee sets his ball down quick and hits it. It lands in a bunker. He was angry because of the circumstances; I was angry because I thought we were going to be robbed of the Open.

The wind was against us, but that proved in our favour because Jacklin couldn't reach the green in two. I'm expecting him to chip-up and two-putt for a five (the 17th was a par-5), so I'm thinking we have to do the same in reverse. I say to Lee, 'Make a five. It's not lost yet.' He's in a pot bunker and it's going to be difficult to get out, but I want him to get out beyond Jacklin's drive so he's second to play. I'm just trying to keep his feet on the ground and try to make up the yardage, but Lee hits out of the bunker and thinks it has all left him. He hits his third into the rough. I don't want him to lose all sense of proportion; we must make a five. Even if we drop a shot because Jacklin makes four, it still keeps us in the Open. With a hole to play, a birdie to a par can square it up again.

Lee was angry. He told Tony the Open was all his. Jacklin had pulled up short about 50 or 60 yards from the green — just the sort of position I'd liked to have been in for us; Trevino put his fourth shot through the green. Jacklin watched it bound through. I think he was convinced the green was fast, but maybe he had forgotten we were coming out of the rough and the topspin ran us through the green. He chipped up short. I looked down at Lee's ball. I saw the lie and line, and knowing what he'd done already, I expected him to chip in. I looked at the ball, looked at the pin and thought, 'There's only one place for it to go. In the hole.' It did.

I jumped off the bank I was sitting on and ran for the ball, elated. But Jacklin was still in a position to make birdie, about 12 feet away. He pulled the ball; a sure sign he was choking. Then he missed the one going back. If anyone put Jacklin off at this stage it was me, because I let out a roar

Top: *Severiano Ballesteros sharing his 1984 triumph with Nick de Paul at St Andrews while Bernhard Langer's caddie, Peter Coleman, looks on.*

Bottom: *Dave Musgrove handing over the trusty putter to Seve at Royal Lytham, 1979.*

Above: *Ian Wright working out the yardage for Seve.*

Right: *Cooking up the line: Drake Oddy and Mark Calcavecchia on the green at Royal Troon
1989 — with chef overseeing the proceedings.*

Top: *Willie Aitchison pleading for Lee
Trevino's putt to go in.*

Bottom: *In it goes . . . and off goes the
Trevino hat!*

Right: *Words of encouragement from
Willie as the 1972 Muirfield Open looks
like slipping away from Trevino.*

Top: *Dave Musgrove sharing the glory with Sandy Lyle in the 1985 Open at Sandwich.*

Bottom: *On the way to winning the 1986 Turnberry Open, Pete Bender and a 'still nervous' Greg Norman stretch out.*

Left: *Still together after all these years. Tip Anderson and Arnold Palmer take on another Open.*

*Dave Musgrove and Sandy Lyle deciding how the land lies at Sandwich 1985.*

when Lee's ball went in, and I was keen to get to the 18th. I never thought for a minute we'd come off that green with a shot in hand; maybe one shot behind, never in front.

What followed was the only bit of gamesmanship you could accuse Lee Trevino of. He pulled me to a halt and said, 'Willie, stand here for a minute. Let Tony go on the tee first. He'll be thinking about the bogey he's just made. Then you follow me and hit me with a driver and drop away quickly because I'm going to hit it so fast he won't know where the ball is until it's down the fairway.' That's exactly what he did, which wasn't illegal. He was going to win, and that was that. Jacklin choked again at the last. He should have finished second.

There's been a lot of talk that Lee put Tony off, that the events finished him. I just think Tony Jacklin had reached his peak. If anybody put him off at the 17th it was me jumping up and down. I'll take the blame, but it was unintentional. I didn't have any mixed feelings about Tony being British, because I was there to do a job for Lee Trevino. I'm a professional just like him. I'm there to help beat the other man. If you start to feel sorry enough to let someone else win, you lose your honesty.

The Trevino era has been a special time of my life and he's made me feel special. Lee's role in golf has been entertaining people, treating the game like a stage. He's given them something else back for their money, and I've been glad to be part of it.

# Albert Fyles

*Tom Weiskopf — Royal Troon 1973*

'Tom's swing was poetry in motion. Jack Nicklaus once said to me, "Albert, when Weiskopf knows how good a player he is, we might as well all pack up our clubs and go home." But he had a dark side, too, as I'm sure everybody knows, and Seve Ballesteros couldn't lace Weiskopf's boots when it came to bad temper on the course.'

A speech impediment from an early age has not deterred Albert Fyles. Nor has being the younger brother of Alfie, the most successful British Open caddie in this era. Albert has scorned a stammer that he will tell you has got him into trouble on more than one occasion on the golf course; and he emerged from brother Alfie's shadow to partner his own Open champion — a player who at one time was reputed to throw a 5-iron almost as long as he could hit it, and who, it was told, sometimes sacked two caddies a week — to the prized claret jug.

The first time I saw a golf course it was Royal Birkdale. My father Teddy took me there. He'd retired from caddying at Birkdale when he was eighty-nine — they couldn't persuade him to wind down. He did eighty-two years of caddying and I think he was perhaps the oldest caddie still working before he finally packed it in. He used to take me walking through the ditches in my bare feet, although I was terrified of frogs and newts. I'd stamp up and down as I walked along, and up would pop the balls that had been buried in the sand. He'd flick them out with an old hickory shafted wedge and say, 'Keep going, son.'

I started working as a caddie in 1944 when I was about eight, and I earned a penny for every year. I had to give up caddying when I left school to take up other jobs, but carrying the bags was in my blood and by the time I was twenty-four I was back to caddying full-time.

Alfie, Ted Halsall, Bobby (Jacky) Lee and myself all lived in Suffolk Road, within a wedge of each other. Alfie was ten years older and Bobby was the youngest, but we all worked up at Birkdale together. In the early 1960s I remember caddying for Brian Huggett and Peter Butler, but in those days we caddied for many players. There were no yardages in those days, and caddies were sacked right, left and centre for pulling wrong clubs. Your player used to test you on the first hole. You had to produce the right club, and if you made a mistake it was the end of you. And we used to do thirty-six holes a day; caddie for one player in the morning and then pick up a fresh bag for the afternoon.

I started on the full golf tour, but it soon became a choice of golf or my family. I chose my family, and just waited for the big boys to come up to the Birkdale area. When we were young we all dreamed of being assistant professionals. My one ambition had been to be a pro, and I got to ten handicap. But there were eight in my family, so we couldn't afford for me to be a pro — they didn't get paid! But with being a keen golfer, I developed a keen eye for a golf ball and a distance. I became a very good eyeballer, and I could read any line on any green.

I didn't have any regular bags in the years leading up to Tom Weiskopf because there were only a few tournaments I could go to. If it meant being away from the family for more than a week it was out. I did have one fairly regular customer though, and it was amazing how we started off. We were lucky to last more than the first fairway together. It was the Carling tournament at Royal Birkdale, a big event with a great deal of money as first prize. I was introduced to Butch Baird from America by a player called Howard King. When I met Butch I just couldn't believe it — he stuttered worse than me! As he walked on to the first tee he couldn't get any proper words out at all, and so I was frightened to speak to him in case he thought I was teasing him. We had no yardages then, and Butch did manage to get out; 'You know the course, don't you, Albert?' I just nodded my head.

Butch hit a decent shot down the first, and then turned round to ask me about his second shot. He said, 'What do you think, Albert?' I knew it was a 3-iron, but could I get the words out? I said, 'It's a th–th–th–' and I whipped the 3-iron out of the bag. 'Are you taking the ****?', growled Butch. He was going to sack me on the spot. I just couldn't get a word out then, I was just a quivering, stuttering heap, and I tried to say, 'I've g–g–g–g– got a sp–sp–sp–speech impediment.' He looks at me and still wonders if I'm fooling. Then he whips round to Howard and says, 'Out of all the caddies you could have chosen, you find me one with a stutter!'

Well, we really got on well together, and when the bell rang for the first round we went on to the first tee and an of-ficial is there to check out which clubs and what type of ball Butch is using. He says to Butch, 'Mr Baird, what type of ball are you using?' Butch tries to answer him but can only say. 'A Ta–Ta–Ta–Ta . . . because he can't get the word Tit-leist out. The official warns Butch he must tell him the type of ball, and so Butch has another go: 'Ta–Ta–Ta–Ta . . .' and he stamps his foot in frustration. The official's following him around with his book as Butch is saying, 'It's a Ta–ta–ta–ta . . ..' All the while I'm thinking, 'Please don't come to me!' Sure enough he does, and says, 'I can't wait for Mr Baird any longer. What ball is he using, caddie?' I say, 'A Ta–Ta–Ta–Ta . . ., and with that he drops his book and stomps off the tee. My speech impediment makes people think I'm a bag of nerves, but it's not true. And I'm glad Tom Weiskopf soon understood that.

I went up to the 1970 Open at St Andrews on spec with a few players in mind but no firm bag. Because he didn't think his player was coming over, Orville Moody's caddie had taken Tom Weiskopf's bag, but when he suddenly heard Orville was flying over, he ditched Tom and suggested I take over the bag. Weiskopf played a regular four-ball with Jack Nicklaus, Tony Jacklin and Bert Yancey, and so I followed this four up to the tee. Because 'Big T', Tom, had got a very bad record for sacking caddies, I was very apprehensive. I could see right away Tom was looking for his caddie, and so I thought, 'This is it — do or die.' I tried to say, 'I've come in your caddie's place', but I couldn't get it all out. Tom thunders, 'Who the hell are *you*?', and I try to tell him I'm Albert Fyles and I've come to take the place of his regular caddie. But I was so nervous I couldn't get it out properly. Tom turns his head in embarrassment and has it explained to him that his regular caddie has gone back to Orville Moody, and I'm his new one, so he says, 'OK', and walks on to the first tee.

When he's on the tee he asks Tony Jacklin if he knows me, and Tony says, 'Yes. He stutters, but he caddied for me for five years and he knows the game inside out. You've got a good one there.' Well, after asking me for yardages, which I didn't have, Tom tested me out. Going down the second fairway he told me he'd lost his yardage book and asked me what I thought his second shot was. What had I got in mind? I was good at eyeballing and so I said, 'A 5-iron', and he hit his second shot right on to the green. He never said another word until the end when he told me he would be going out at 8 AM with the same four-ball and he would see me then.

We played three more rounds in the same four-ball until the bell rang (it was time to start the tournament proper). When the bell did ring, I soon found a different Tom Weiskopf. I was under terrible pressure straight away. Tom was like a wild man, kicking bags and throwing clubs. All the stories I'd read about him and heard about him from other caddies were true! By the third tee I was really worried. Tom's wife (a former beauty queen) could see I was worried sick. She said, 'Don't worry, Albert. Take no notice of him. He does it all the time. He sacks two caddies a week in the States.' 'Thanks, Mrs Weiskopf,' I said, wondering how long I was going to last. We made the cut, but he was so bad-tempered he wouldn't speak to me, and sometimes I just didn't know what to do for the best.

I felt, at the time, it was such a shame. Tom's temper stopped him reaching his true potential. Everyone knew he had all the attributes a golfer needs, and his swing was poetry in motion. He was such a perfectionist. He wouldn't allow for mistakes, he used to take it out of himself, his equipment — and, of course, the nearest guy at hand. That happened to be me.

I remember one British Open at Turnberry, we were playing the 16th and Tom had been in a burn. He put his next in the sand and there was this photographer taking shots of Tom. Tom played a bad shot out of the bunker, and he does no more than charge straight at this press guy. I had to take his sand-iron off him because he was threatening the guy with it. He really took it out of this photographer, and I can tell you he's lucky to be alive today. Well, the crowd didn't like that and they really booed Tom. Tom then hit his tee-shot in a fury and he struck it further than I go on holidays. The 17th is a par-5 of 500 yards or more, but Tom reduced it to a drive and a sand-iron! You could smell rubber burning. To give some idea of just how long Tom Weiskopf could hit a ball — and he was the longest driver of his time — Tommy Horton, who was playing with us, needed a driver and 4-iron at the 17th. At the time, Peter Alliss said it was the longest drive he'd seen in his life. I know why.

But Tom was a great character, a McEnroe of golf. He didn't know what he was going to do next. And if he played a bad shot, he let the spectators know about it. They hated him but loved him.

We made the cut in 1970 for my first British Open with

Tom, but a bad last round put him down the field. In 1971 I was hoping for great things, because the British Open was at Birkdale, my home-course, but Tom couldn't handle Birkdale. A lot of the great players couldn't. Tom didn't break par more than once or twice at Birkdale. We made the cut in 1971, but we finished way down the field.

In 1972 Tom's temper had got worse and worse and I felt like packing it in, as we finished seventh at Muirfield, the year Tony Jacklin should have won and Lee Trevino did. But at the later part of the season Tom wrote to me and said he'd got an invitation for the Piccadilly World Match-play at Wentworth. I'd no idea how he'd got the invite because it was supposed to be a tournament for the top eight players in the world, and he hadn't reached that standard. He beat Lee Trevino in the final three and two. Bearing in mind Trevino had beaten Tony Jacklin, despite Jacklin shooting a 62, this was a great achievement by Tom. It set him up for next year, I'm sure. By the time he arrived for Troon for the 1973 British Open, he'd calmed down altogether; he couldn't do enough for me. I was seeing a different Tom again.

Tom came over eight days before the 1973 British Open started and he played his first two practice rounds with that great Australian golfer Bruce Crampton. This was the start of the most gruelling week of my life. Soon the regular four-ball of Weiskopf, Nicklaus, Jacklin and Yancey were playing together. In all, we played two to three rounds of golf most days and then off to the practice paddock. We played 12 or 13 rounds of golf before the bell rang, starting at 8.30 AM and finishing at 9 PM, for seven days. I was worked until my legs bowed. I was a big guy in those days and my legs swelled up. I was sharing a place with Bobby (Jacky) Lee and Ted Halsall in the Portland Hotel, and they had to help me out of bed when the bell rang. I never thought I'd make it. How I got round for the four days of the tournament, I don't know. I've seen the video tape of Tom and I coming down the 18th. Tom's got his arm around me, hugging me, and the commentator says, 'Look at the smile on that caddie's face. No wonder, he's just bringing home the British Open champion.' Little did he know that it wasn't a smile, but a grimace of pain. I was gritting my teeth, thinking, 'Thank god we're going down the 18th.'

I don't think any other caddie in the history of the British Open has worked harder than I did that week. There were some light-hearted moments in practice with the big four, though. The Tarbuck ice-cream incident, for instance. Jimmy Tarbuck and his mate Kenny Lynch followed us around for one of the practice days and, unusually for Tom and I, it was a sunny day. So Tarbuck asked us all if we'd like an ice-cream. He said he'd pay, and despatched Kenny Lynch, who didn't seem too pleased with the idea, I must say, to fetch the ice-creams. It's a fair way off to the ice-cream cart so when Kenny comes back he's got ice-cream cones melting all down his arms. He tried to duck under the ropes to come over to us, but gets stopped by a security man who asks him what he's playing at. Kenny tells the guy he's with the group, so the security man calls out to Jimmy, did he know who Kenny was? Jimmy says, 'I've never seen him before in my life.' I thought Jack Nicklaus was going to choke. He was killing himself with laughing, but dashed over to the security man and put Kenny out of his misery.

For the first round it was a nice day in the morning, but we were out in late afternoon and we played eighteen holes in drizzle. The local weather forecaster had told me we'd get rain and we did. We got it for all the tournament. Tom played out of his skin. A 68 in the rain, 4 under par was brilliant. He only missed three greens out of the eighteen, and he putted like crazy. Actually, in the whole four rounds that week, he never three-putted once. The greens weren't at their best that year either. And, as the rain got worse during the rounds I thought someone was going to have to go off and build an ark. As well as Tom's putting, he played the key holes at Troon really well. For instance, the 8th, the

Postage Stamp: Tom birdied it twice and parred it twice. He didn't do as well as Gene Sarazen in the first round at the Postage Stamp, though. Gene was playing right behind us with Max Faulkner and Harry Bradshaw, I think, and he got his famous hole-in-one. We didn't see the ball go in because we were on the 9th tee, but we heard hell of a din behind and Tom said, 'Some guy must have holed out.' Some guy, all right. And Peter Oosterhuis had taken an eight or nine there some time earlier! Tom only missed the Postage Stamp green once during the tournament, and then he chipped up stone dead. In my eyes it's the hardest hole on the course. A lot of championships have been won and lost there.

We played the 11th, the par-5 by the railway, really well all week too. We birdied that twice and parred twice. And the 17th we got to grips with each time, the long short hole. Playing these holes well made the difference. We played with Gary Player for the first two rounds and he was as miserable as sin about our luck with the weather because we caught it again for the second round. It was a bad day. The wind blew and it rained very heavily. Tom shot a 67. With Brian Barnes it was the best of the day. Incredible. Tom wouldn't wear rain gear because he couldn't find a set to really fit his 6ft 3in frame, so it was hard work for me to keep him dry. I had the umbrella up all the time.

We just seemed to time it wrong with the weather. If we went out in the morning it was raining and fine in the afternoon, and then it rained when we went out in the after-noon after a fine morning. We couldn't win. He was so unlucky with the weather and I thought it would dishearten him, but he just kept going. Knowing how highly strung he was, everyone was waiting for him to crack — including me — but this was a different Tom. It was the best round of golf for conditions like those I'd ever seen, or have seen since. He got out the 1-iron and drilled the ball low all the way round. He made that 1-iron talk, hitting it below the wind. It was his number-one weapon in more than one sense. He could hit it as far as a 3-wood — and it won him the 1973 Open.

With Troon built horse-shoe shaped, the wind was never the same. One minute it was left-to-right, the next right-to-left, so you had to keep the ball low. Johnny Miller hit his shots high, ballooned them, and that was no good this year. It cost him the tournament. It was a quiet round as well. Tom never spoke much to Gary. He was in contention, you see. Tom doesn't speak much to anyone but to the caddie when he's in contention and he marches off at a cracking pace. He told me, 'You don't speak a word to anybody else, and when I've hit that ball, we're on our way.' I maintain that's how he turned over Lee Trevino in the World Matchplay. He just wouldn't hold a conversation with him. I remember Lee saying, 'What's up, Tom?' and Tom says, 'I don't want to talk.' Lee says, 'Well, you can listen, can't you?'

Anyway, we spent the whole round with Tom stomping off and me scurrying alongside him trying to keep up. That did my poor legs a world of good, of course. But a 67 and he slept well that night. We shot a 71 in the third round, still under par. In fact he was under par each day and he led the tournament from start to finish and equalled the Championship four-round score. In appalling conditions, that was remarkable.

Johnny Miller played with us for the last two days. He was our biggest danger in the end, although I thought it was going to be Tom's four-ball partner Bert Yancey who might prove the biggest threat. He'd played well in practice. I had first-hand experience of that. Bert had shot two 69s after playing with Jack Nicklaus in the first two rounds, and Jack was, of course in contention. Jack faded out of it with a 76 in the third round, though, and then had that fantastic 65 in the last round — all too late. Well, by the time things had sorted themselves out, Johnny Miller was nearest to us and we were paired with him. They shook hands on the tee for the fourth round and said, 'Have a good round' to each other. Then I don't think they spoke another word to each other for the rest of the round. Just as we set off, would you believe it, the heavens opened. We started one stroke ahead of Miller, but it was all-square after the second where we missed the green and bogeyed. That was as near as anyone got to beating Tom. Up ahead Neil Coles was putting together a 66, which eventually saw him tie with Johnny, but by the fifth or sixth, when we'd picked up a couple of birdies to Johnny's pars or bogey, I thought, 'This is our Open.' Johnny did fight back but the old 1-iron killed him off. We got a birdie at the 11th by using the 1-iron when Johnny went for the 3-wood, got on, but not near enough to make the birdie putt. He got one back on us at the 15th to put him three shots behind again, so the 17th was going to be a crucial hole. It's over 220 yards, of course, and it had been playing long all week. With the wind against, it was certainly playing long in the last round. We decided we weren't going to get on without flirting with a lot of trouble, so we opted for the trusty 1-iron again. Johnny hit a 3-wood well right. He chipped-up and made par. Tom was 12 yards short on the apron, so he putted — and he putted stone dead.

I patted the three tees in my pocket as we walked to the 18th tee. Tom's very superstitious and he used to make me carry three tees in my pocket. I had to have those three tees when I walked off the 18th. He'd want to see them. I tapped them once more for luck. We were three shots ahead, so perhaps Tom didn't need that much luck this time. We took out the 1-iron on the tee. I don't think we used the timber more than five times in the whole round. It left us no more than a 7-iron into the green. Johnny was desperate. He drove right, and then, playing his last dice, hit his second into the bunker. I knew what was going through Tom's mind. He had his eye on Arnold Palmer's record. He knew if he birdied the last he'd break it. That worried me. I couldn't see him throwing it away, but I didn't want him to give himself the chance. This is where a good caddie has to speak his mind. I could tell he was thinking about Arnold's 276 when he said to me, 'What have you got in mind, Albert?' He had to be desperate to ask. It didn't happen many times him asking me to club him. We normally decided together, if anything. I don't think I ever gave him a wrong 'un, though.

The pin was on the right at the back of a bunker and I decided on the 7-iron. I said to Tom, 'There's no record to be broken; just play for the heart of the green.' He hit the green and turned round to me, patted me on the back, and said, 'Thanks for thinking for me, Albert.' He was pin high to the left of the flag and the crowd was stamping and cheering as we walked down to the green. Tom put his arm on my shoulder and said, with tears in his eyes, 'There's one man I'd dearly love to be in that stand — my daddy.' His father had died that year.

In went the putt and he asked me to keep the ball because he wanted to take it home and get it mounted instead of throwing it to the crowd. It was a small Slazenger, the last small ball to win a British Open. Tom equalled the championship record of 276 with a 70 and I thought it would be a long time before it would be broken. Tom Watson proved me wrong only four years later. I was over the moon for Tom, but I was also cold, wet, and in agony with my legs. Tom could see this so he gave me the key to his hotel room and told me to have a shower and put on some of his clothes. They were a bit big for me but they were lovely and dry and I was feeling great when he came in with a bottle of champagne. It was even better when I got a hug and a kiss from the former Miss Minnesota!

# Nick de Paul

'As we came off the 17th green Seve said, "There's going to be a playoff." I said, "If we birdie the last there won't be any need for a playoff." I think it got him thinking positive. That's exactly what he did and he won the British Open."'

Pennsylvanian Nick de Paul will be forever known as the man who could always catch Severiano Ballesteros out. In fact Nick, twice a major winner with Seve, the 1983 US Masters and the 1984 British Open at St Andrews, could, and still can, catch anyone out.

Nick is the man with the baseball glove who can stand at the end of the practice range and catch his master's ball no matter whether it has been struck with a sand-iron or a driver. He pouches the ball with the eye of a major league outfielder, and that is because he was a player of some repute before he gave up the bat for the bag at the start of the 1970s. He has brightened up practice for his pros and armies of spectators, from Augusta to Wentworth, with his baseball trick. But he is no circus act: as well as the major double, Nick carried Seve's bag to ten other tour victories to become one of the most respected caddies in golf.

After coming into caddying quite late in life — when he was thirty years old — Nick, who used to be a baseball player and was 'quite good at it', perfected his catching trick with his first professional, George Archer, who lived on a farm.

We had all this practice ground out there — just cornfields and Hereford cattle — acres of space to hit balls. So I used to get George's game in shape in a hurry by providing a target out in the field. When I caught all the balls it made the game a lot more fun for both of us. My ultimate desire — as it was with Seve and all my pros — was the perfect bag; catching every ball without letting one hit the ground, from a wedge to a driver. You'd be surprised how much relaxation this provides; just the thing for warming up before the British Open!

❁ ❁ ❁

*Nick warmed up his caddie career from 1971 to 1974 carrying Archer's bag, and then moved on to work for Australian Bruce Crampton until 1977, when he moved on to another Australian, Graham Marsh. Nick stayed with Marsh for four years, but as the Australian started to wind down his US operation, the baseball-glove specialist looked for pastures new. Nick's reputation had been noticed by a Spaniard who had taken the golfing world by storm to win the 1979 British Open, Seve Ballesteros.*

❁ ❁ ❁

In 1981 Seve asked me if I'd do a few tournaments with him when he came to the States. He'd won the 1979 Open and I knew what kind of player he was so I was pretty thrilled about being asked. He was a real demanding guy, as everybody knows, but what we caddies liked about him was his determination. We knew he was going to try his hardest for 72 holes. He had such a lot of natural talent to go with this. Even if you were five behind with five to go with Seve, he still thought he could win, and there's nothing pumps a caddie up more than a guy who thinks like that.

❁ ❁ ❁

*The 1984 British Open may well go down as the Open that was lost by two players as much as it was won by Severiano Ballesteros. But it will certainly be remembered as having one of the most exciting finishes for years. Australian Ian Baker-Finch, an unknown player featuring in his first British Open, slipped up right at the start of the last day, hitting his second shot into the Swilcan Burn. Tom Watson from the US was bidding for the joint record-sixth British Open victory that would make him immortal alongside Harry Vardon. His bid started to go wrong at the 12th hole and spluttered out at the 17th, the Road Hole, where many an aspiration had been snuffed out in the past. While they were being pinned back by the Old Course, one man was able to deliver the coup-de-grâce to St Andrews with a birdie finish, gently cajoled by an American renowned for catching golf balls in a baseball glove.*

@ @ @

I should have had a bet on Seve before the Open. I could have got odds of ten to one and made a fortune. He was playing so well at The Belfry (Lawrence Batley International) in his practice rounds, especially, that I should have known he was going to do something special. You could get the odds because he'd had a poor year until then by his standards. While he didn't score very well at The Belfry, you could see he was tuning up. His game was coming together. I reckoned St Andrews was a hooker's course, as well, all the trouble is on the right. It was just made for Seve.

As it was, I nearly didn't get the chance to make a start with Seve. We were at The Belfry the week before and I was due to fly from there up to St Andrews directly after the event. It was only a four-seater plane, though, and in the end there wasn't enough room for me, so I had to take a bus from Birmingham up to Dundee. The night I went up the bus wasn't due to leave until 11 PM, so I left my luggage with the bus station and went for a meal. When I got back I found the office wasn't open until the next day, so I had to get a driver to break in for me. It was a good job he did. I couldn't go without the gear, so I'd have missed the first day. As it was, I arrived about 9 AM at St Andrews and had time to walk round the course and refresh my memory. I'd caddied there in 1978, but I needed to get the feel and my bearings.

I needn't have worried too much because Seve was in complete control on the first round. It was if he was at home at St Andrews. He hardly put a foot wrong in the first round and I can't remember once having to discuss a club or study a line with him. If the others had realized just how totally in charge he was I think they would have been very jittery. He shot a 69, three-under-par, and although it wasn't leading, it didn't change my thinking that he was going to be there at the finish.

@ @ @

*Leading after day one were Australia's Greg Norman and Peter Jacobsen from the US, who had shot rounds of 67. Ian Baker-Finch returned a 68 and jumped into the lead after a second round 66 put him three strokes ahead of Nick Faldo, Lee Trevino and Ballesteros. Tom Watson came into the reckoning after also carding a 66 in the third round. This left him tied on 205 for the three rounds with Baker-Finch, who shot 71 on the third day. Ballesteros returned 70 for day three to be two strokes behind the two leaders, with the West German Bernhard Langer. This meant that Watson and Baker-Finch would be the last pairing out, following Langer and Ballesteros.*

@ @ @

We woke up to yet another fine day for the last round. I was relieved because I knew Seve would play his best with the sun on his back.

Bernhard Langer got the first blow in by hitting a great second shot over the Swilcan Burn at the first hole to only a few inches, about a foot I guess, and birdied to go one nearer the lead. Pete Coleman was caddying for Bernhard, and Pete had caddied for Seve, for a time, so he was thinking it was one-up to them. I thought, 'Things are going to be tight this afternoon,' and I know Seve was thinking the same. But a little matter of a birdie for Bernhard wasn't going to unsettle Seve, and he got straight back to the job, hitting some lovely shots to the green. The putts didn't seem to want to drop, though. We did get a birdie at the 5th and got back at Bernhard, and that seemed to put Seve in good spirit. The important thing was that we were closer to the lead.

Baker-Finch had had an unlucky start by spinning back into the burn at the 1st, and when I checked the leaderboard we were a stroke behind Watson with Langer, so there was all to play for.

I knew a putt would have to drop before long and it came at the 8th, the par-3 (178 yards). Seve hit a great tee-shot and left himself an eight-foot putt. He sank it and turned to me with a real glint in his eye and said something like, 'Now let's go.' He was relieved to see one go in. The 10-footers wouldn't go in, though. He just couldn't get a decent length to putt to fall, and I felt it was getting to him. I tried to help out by looking at the putts, but he still didn't really need me. What he needed was a bit of luck on the roll.

We got just the opposite at the 11th, where we dropped a shot and went back to 10 under. It's a short hole, 172 yards, and Seve left it short. We both thought an 8-iron would be enough with the wind, but it needed a club more. It made it worse when we knew Watson had picked up a shot here. But then as we played the 13th I thought it might just be down to Bernhard and Seve. Baker-Finch had slipped off the leaderboard, and Watson looked to be in big trouble with his drive at the 12th.

Tom never should have taken a driver because there's a lot of trouble near the hole (316 yards, par-4). I think he'd tried to make a certain birdie but he'd really come unstuck. He'd hit into the heavy gorse and I honestly thought he was going to take a seven. Somehow he managed only a bogey-five, and he got the shot back straight away at the 13th. We stayed right with him, though, because at last Seve dunked in a long one. It was all of 25 feet at the 14th (567 yards, par-5) and that was a real lift for us both. At last we'd sunk a decent putt. We were level but it was playing on my nerve-ends. I don't know what it was doing to Seve, but he looked mighty determined.

My nerves were really jangling when we got to the

17th, the Road Hole. Each day so far we'd driven into the left rough and finished up taking bogey-fives. Three fives, and they were all great bogey-fives. Each one of them could have been double-bogeys or worse! I wasn't absolutely brimming with confidence but there was nothing wrong with Seve's tee-shot this time. What a cool customer! I can't even remember the length of the putt for par, I was so relieved to be away from the hole without any damage. We'd made our first four of the week there and that was that. Relief. Now I think about it afterwards, the Road Hole was definitely the turning point of the Open for both Watson and Ballesteros. I guess it wasn't the first tournament to be won and lost on the Road Hole at St Andrews.

As we came off the 17th green Seve said, 'There's going to be a playoff.' I said, 'If we birdie the last there won't be any need for a playoff.' I think that got him thinking positive. That's exactly what he did and he won the British Open. I looked behind. I'm not sure whether Seve did, and I saw Watson in trouble, having gone through the green and up against the wall. Seve hit a perfect drive at the last, left-centre of the fairway. He then only needed a pitching-wedge and he hit it straight at the pin to about 18 feet or so. I thought it was even closer when he hit it because it was covering the flag all the way. I'll never forget the last putt as long as I live. It was a right-to-left turn up the hill and he hit it perfectly all the way — or so I thought. To me it seemed to hang on the right lip for at least two seconds before it dropped in. People tell me it wasn't anything like that sort of time. Anyway, when it fell there was an almighty roar. Seve was very excited, and it must have had an effect on Watson. He had a big putt to hole on the 17th and he didn't make it. There was no way we could lose now. Seve was even more excited.

It was time for me to disappear. I wanted Seve to have the stage to himself — he'd earned it. He'd got to have his moment. He's quite a guy. I hope somewhere down the line I'll have the opportunity of carrying the sack again for him.

# Dave Musgrove

*Severiano Ballesteros — Royal Lytham & St Annes 1979*
*Sandy Lyle — Royal St Georges 1985 Sandwich*

'The difference between Sandy and Seve? Well, the night after Sandy won his Open he was in the marquee, which was holding his celebration dinner, with his apron on, cleaning up and wishing everybody would go so he could get some peace and quiet. Straight after *his* Open win, Seve had vanished on another crusade, to beat another army, and save another universe.'

Penetrate a fairly gruff exterior, and you will find Dave Musgrove, at one time Seve Ballesteros' right-hand man and now caddying for Sandy Lyle, an affable philosopher, who will trot out an occasional quotation, from Shakespeare to Dylan. The quote will fit the occasion, such as the following lines from Rudyard Kipling, Dave's favourite analogy for carrying the top player's bags:

> *If you can meet with Triumph and Disaster*
> *And treat those two imposters just the same,*

*You'll be a caddie my son!*

*Since 1955, when he was 12 years old and first picked up the bag, Dave has had plenty of chance to come up against those two impostors. While his friends were earning their few pennies for a week's work as paper-boys and butcher's assistants, Dave was caddying for a round at Hollinwell, the championship course near his home. Picking up tips did not just come in the form of money, for Dave learned enough to become a single-figure handicap golfer by 1967. Today he plays off a nine handicap, a great help when he is carrying the bag.*

*Top-line caddying was at first only part-time for Dave, although even a part-time career brought him face to face with the second of the* twin imposters, disaster, in 1971 at the Open championship at Royal Birkdale. Perhaps it was not so much disaster as disappointment. Dave was caddying for Roberto de Vicenzo, who looked as though he could win his second Open, but he hit two great shots and then three-putted the 13th in the third round.

After a few years caddying on and off for de Vicenzo, Dave went into full-time caddying in the mid-1970s, although he was still doing work other than caddying when he took the bag of Vicente Fernandez. Fernandez, as he was to do some years later, provided a link to Dave's caddying days with one Severiano Ballesteros. Dave's first major success with Fernandez came at Fulford in 1975 when the Argentinian clinched the Benson and Hedges International. Also at the tournament were Manuel and Severiano Ballesteros, who was in his first year on the tour, and only eighteen years old. In 1976 Dave was supposed to be caddying for Fernandez at the French Open, but Vicente had broken his finger, so he was without a bag — until Manuel Ballesteros asked him if he would like to carry for his brother Seve. That was the start of a four-year relationship.

@ @ @

Roberto had written and asked me to carry for him in that year's Open. Loads of people had let him down over the years, so I didn't want to be one of them. I got my mate to caddie for Seve. Seve finished second to Johnny Miller and after that I caddied for him until the end of 1979. Even in the 1975 Open Roberto recognized how good Seve was, at Lytham in 1979 he told me Seve was going to win, and before the 1976 Open he said, 'There's Johnny Miller, Tom Weiskopf and Seve. All the rest of us are just here to make up the numbers.' My gut reaction was the same.

I first saw Seve at the PGA Championship, which he won, at Royal St Georges in 1975. He was lashing away at balls on the practice ground. I saw long legs and a big pair of hands and he was standing a long way from the ball, giving himself plenty of room. I saw the name on the bag and asked his age and I was astounded. He continued to astound me for the next four years. They were difficult years, and I felt I'd served my sentence when we parted company.

⊘ ⊘ ⊘

*Seve had just the right sort of build-up to the 1979 Open at Lytham: he won the English Classic at The Belfry, the first time it was played, and then he came second in the Scandinavian Open in Sweden.*

⊘ ⊘ ⊘

The Belfry was cold and wet, which gave us a taste of what was to come at Lytham. The fairways were worse than they are now. Say what you like about the Ryder Cup and The Belfry, if it wasn't for the 9th, 10th and 18th holes, it would be as average as it looks. The 10th fairway was covered in clover and the ball was uncontrollable. On the hole you either finished in the back bunker or short, in the water. Seve won under par. I remember one day on the 8th there was a little dinghy turned over on the lake and he hooked his tee-shot, hit the boat and came out on the fairway — the shape of things to come!

We went to Sweden to play the Scandinavian Enterprise Open and he played well there, but Sandy won it. Ironic that, because Seve won an event and Sandy came second in it, just before the 1985 Open.

We had a week off in between and then it was the Lytham Open. Seve was playing and competing well. He should have been on a real high, but you can never tell with Seve. When he wins he turns up the next week as if nothing's happened — and as if he hasn't got a penny to his name, that's the difference between Seve and others — what sets him apart a bit, I suppose. Winning can destroy a lot of people. The occasion and the competition never bothers Seve; it's the same with the course he might be playing. It can be the worst layout imaginable, but he'll go into it 100 percent. He never worries about winning or who he plays with. Seve treats everybody exactly the same; they're all there as fellow competitors and he doesn't bat an eyelid at who he plays with. He didn't when he was eighteen and he didn't in 1979 at Lytham. He doesn't now, whether they've been a super star for a long time or if he's never heard of them. He knows they can all play well or badly — and they can all be beaten. If you can walk with kings and keep the common touch . . .

At Birkdale in 1976 for instance, somebody asked him in the press tent if he was worried about playing with Johnny Miller (the eventual champion). His brother was interpreting and he answered for Seve saying, 'We can go out now and play.' He meant it. Those early press conferences showed another side to him. He used to be asked long, drawn-out questions that went on and on. Manuel would appear to be explaining to him forever and then Seve would seem to be replying forever. When Manuel gave his reply he would often just say, 'Yes!'

In 1979 Seve seemed to be giving 101 percent. Roberto waited for him every morning and they practised putting before playing their practice rounds together. Roberto offered Seve some great advice: 'You have to know what it's like on these links. When the wind changes it's as if you have never played the hole before. It can change in its nature so much.'

Although he was hitting the ball all over the place in practice, Seve was figuring out which side of the fairways to miss on a lot of holes, and places where he couldn't go at all. He found loopholes in the rough, if you like. He knew there were certain places you could go and have a chance. There was no fluke to Seve's play out of the rough in the 1979 Open; he knew what he was doing all right.

In the first round we teed-off with Ken Brown and Lee Trevino. It was the coldest week imaginable for so-called summer; Trevino still had his pyjamas on underneath his golf gear! In those days Seve just hit the ball as hard as he could. He'd stand there and lash at it and then expect to hole every putt. In the second round he shot a 65. He came back in 31. He birdied 14 and chipped in at 15, and so I thought if he can birdie 16 he might shoot 69. But he didn't. He lipped out . . . and birdied 17 and 18 for a 65! The point is, though, no matter how badly people might say he played that week and won — everybody's going to miss a few fairways; Tom Watson was just as erratic in 1983, that's his game and he's no mug — he'd got it all worked out.

The next two rounds we played with Hale Irwin, who was leading the tournament. Nobody talks much about Irwin, nowadays, and he doesn't sell himself. I think he's a good fellow. Straight. A lot was said at the time. He was made out to be the bad guy playing against Seve, especially after one of their clashes at Wentworth in the World Match-play, but I don't know. Seve's always been convinced the Americans have got it in for him, anyway, but he's said that about the French, the Italians, the Japanese. Anyway, if you look at Irwin's last two round scores — 75–78 — they weren't going to beat anybody. Both Seve and Irwin played badly in the third round, but you're never going to do a good score at Lytham when it feels like three degrees below freezing and there's a gale blowing, are you? Everybody was wrapped up like it was the Arctic. You couldn't feel your hands. And Seve's back was a real pain — the cold got to it and it troubled him so much that we had to go and find a physiotherapist.

Well, they both got it around in 75 and the crowd was on Seve's side good and proper. They were all behind him, shouting 'get in' even when he missed a putt by six feet. It looked good. On the last day Seve birdied the first hole and Hale took a six on the second, I can remember the scoring because in those days I had to mark all the cards, and I re-member putting Irwin down for a six — and then the card blew in to the bunker on the second and I had to go chasing after it.

As well as Seve's good start on the fourth round, he also birdied one of the par-5s going out and that put him in front. Then they all started challenging — Isao Aoki, Rodger Davis, Crenshaw and Nicklaus. It's a strange thing; you don't usually see the tournament. You can only see your one match, only your two players. Most of the time you have no idea what's happening anywhere else. You see a name come up on the leaderboard, then it might disappear and you think to yourself, 'I wonder what happened to him?', and you forget him after a while. You hear the crowd roar and a new name comes up on the leaderboard and you wonder whether he holed a long putt or chipped in. Was the board wrong? It never is, though, at the Open. Anyway, Aoki came and went; Crenshaw came up; Davis came up, but then he double-bogeyed the 14th, I think. We did know that, at least. Seve just kept hacking along. On the 6th hole he says, 'It is him with the biggest heart who will win.' He meant he'd got the bottle.

What happened at the 13th is put down to fortune. People tie it in with the fact that Jack Nicklaus was unlucky not to win. Maybe he was unlucky on the last day, but on the first day he holed-in-one at the 5th and Seve hadn't even started. Then on the second day, Nicklaus puts it stone-dead at the 5th and so he's taken just three shots for the 5th! You have to think about what's happened every day in a Championship. You take your luck as it happens.

But the killer shot certainly was at the 13th when Seve drove into the bunker. He was going for the green on the short par-4. He'd tried loads of different clubs but this time he said, 'We'll go for it today.' I ask you: just twenty-one years old, leading the Open, six holes to go and he's going for the green! He hit it into the hill and the ball caught the top of the bunker and went in 60 yards from the flag. He came out with a fantastic shot, but it screwed off to the right of the green, and went down off the mound instead of falling in towards the flag. He then holed it for a three. To birdie with a long par-4 coming up was a great bonus when he might have expected to bogey.

He three-putted the 14th, and then the television

buggy came past on its way to the 15th, and the guys on board told me that Crenshaw — who was nearest challenger then — had double-bogeyed 17. Seve always wants to know what's going on. If you can tell him what's happening with the other players he's happy because then he knows what there is to do. Those that aren't winners don't want to know what's happening to anybody else. As soon as they see their names on the leaderboard they worry themselves to death until their name's gone off the board. Then they're all right again. I said to Seve, 'Crenshaw's just double-bogeyed the 17th.' 'Oh,' he says, then smashes the ball off the 15th tee, up over the hill and goes running after it down the other side. His second shot was in the rough on the left, but a long way down and then he chips stone-dead.

At the 16th there's a tractor-path between two fairways where they park the cars. Seve's drive was 50 yards from the front of the green and about 40 yards from the middle of the Open course fairway, but he was on the right side — don't forget all his careful planning on studying the rough beforehand — which means he's now coming back into the wind. From the fairway you couldn't stop the ball where the flag had been positioned. If you played it out to the left of the fairway it was down-wind and a difficult shot.

He walked up to the green and found a spot to land on. He didn't bother too much where the flag was, he was just interested in where he was going to land the ball. He paced it back and says to me, 'Where is the ball?' I says, 'Under the car somewhere.' Then they all sorted out where he could drop — on the tractor path, which was in effect fairway. He hammers the ball at the green, lands on the bit he wanted to stop on about 15 to 20 feet from the hole. Then he holes the putt, and I knew he'd won because he was three shots in front. He'd hit exactly the tee-shot he wanted to — a high cut to gain maximum distance with the wind and finish on the right. He'd spotted the rough out there wasn't too bad if he'd gone in it. That was the way to come in; he knew he

could get it on the green from there. No matter what anybody else says, it was all deliberate and planned.

On the 17th the bunkers are on the left, so Seve missed
the fairway to the right and hacks over all the trouble up the
right, pitches on and the crowd are all shouting 'get in'.
They really are all behind him now. It was ten years since
Jacklin had won and they'd adopted Seve. Then there was a
big cheer from the 18th and we thought it was Nicklaus
who'd holed for a birdie. But the board didn't change. We
were puzzled. What had happened was that Mark James,
playing with Nicklaus, had missed the green, shanked his
chip right across the green, and then taken a train ride to get
the putt for a four. But the noise put Seve on his guard and
he played the 17th conservatively, for him. In fact he'd have
been happy with a five.

Now we came to the 18th. The only place, really, you
haven't to go is right — in the bushes. Seve hit a 3-wood and
hooked it miles, nearly on to the first green. He says to me,
'What's over there?' I say, 'I don't know. I've never been
over there.' By this time I'm like the ice-man and he's still at
boiling-point. He hacks forward after asking me if it was a
5-iron. I'd agreed it was. At that stage I'd have agreed to
anything just to get in. It comes up just short of the green,
but he can putt it and he says, 'I can take four putts from
here and still win.' I say, 'No you can't, because I've got a
bet on with one of the caddies that the winning score will be
under par. So you need to make four.' He whacked it up
and got it; I won. Harry Carpenter came up to interview him
and asked him about the last putt. He said, 'My caddie told
me I had to get it.'

There was no great celebrations after Seve's win. Me
and my mother stayed the night at Seve's place and
watched the Open on television. The next morning they'd
all gone.

# DAVE MUSGROVE

*After the 1979 season, Dave caddied for Michael King and Manuel Calero, then he made his first bid for the bag of Sandy Lyle.*

@ @ @

Sandy was going to the US and I asked if I could carry for him the next year, but everybody was asking so I didn't get very far. I still went to the US though, and caddied for Andy North, but I got plenty of chance to talk to Sandy that year (1980) and struck up an acquaintance with him. The following year Calero looked like getting in the Ryder Cup side, but he had to finish in the first two at York (Benson and Hedges International). Sandy was already in the side, and I got talking to him again, Calero was struggling, and I said I might not have a bag for the Ryder Cup. Sandy then asked me if I'd like to carry for him at Walton Heath for the Cup. He had Jimmy Dickinson caddying for him, but Jimmy caddies for Jack Nicklaus in the Ryder Cup. I thought to myself, 'Jimmy Dickinson doesn't go abroad and certainly not to the States, so if I make a good job of it at Walton Heath I might be caddying for Sandy full-time in the future.' That's exactly what happened. I started with Sandy in 1982, full time.

Caddying for Sandy is different again to Seve. Seve wears himself out week after week. He puts so much into it, and expects so much every time. With Sandy things are much more relaxed. It doesn't take so much out of you. After Seve's win at Lytham I was worn out for a week. I didn't feel like that after Sandwich. You can talk to Sandy about lines for putts and which irons. With Seve you're sticking your neck out telling him how far it is to the green. Of the two Opens Sandy never looked like winning until the end; Seve had it won a long way away. The night after Sandy won he was in the marquee that was holding his celebration dinner, with his apron on cleaning up and wishing everybody would go so he could get some peace and quiet. Seve vanished on another crusade, to beat another army, save another universe.

The next time Seve played after his Open win he was at St Mellion and playing the worst he'd played to shoot a 79. It just gave Seve a lot more pressure. It gave Sandy inspiration, the confidence to win the Masters, knowing he was a world-class player. Straight after St Georges he shot a 65 and 64 in the Benson and Hedges, and won it. Then he came second after losing a playoff in the Glasgow Open. Both have got many years of winning left, but you can bet it won't take it out of Sandy the way it does out of Seve.

@ @ @

*If Seve Ballesteros had looked a winner all along in 1979, and certainly looked likely to lift the claret jug from a long way out, Dave's second Open success was not so cut-and-dried. In fact, Sandy Lyle had to emerge from a pack of players at Royal St Georges in 1985 to become the first British winner for years. But the build-up to it had a familiar ring about it for Dave. The only change seemed to be the players, and the places!*

@ @ @

Well, I survived my time with Seve, and in my first full year with Sandy I thought he was going to come up trumps straight away in the Open. He had his chance at Troon in 1982 when Tom Watson won. Sandy played with Watson in the third round, and Tom played so bad he convinced himself he wouldn't win. But then a lot of them fancied their chances that year — Peter Oosterhuis, Nick Faldo, and so on, and Bobby Clampett led for a while and it looked as though they might not be able to catch him. Then there was Nick Price of course.

There was no indication a couple of weeks before the 1985 Open that Sandy was going to do well. In the Irish Open at Royal Dublin, Sandy wanted a four in the first round at the 18th for an 89. He hit his second shot out-of-bounds and walked in. That was the early lead-up to the Open. But then the wind was horrendous at Dublin: the ships in Dublin Bay were bobbing about like corks, and the last man to equal par on that first day had gone out at 11.30 AM. We went out at 2 PM.

The plan was to come home from Ireland, have a week at home, play in the French Open, The Belfry, and then the Open. Because of his Dublin escapade, however, Sandy said he'd have to go to Monte Carlo, the next tournament. It meant me having to dash back to England because my passport was at home, and we'd got no tickets. We finished third in Monte Carlo so things were looking up.

Then it was on to St Germain for the French Open. Seve won it and Sandy came second. It was just the opposite to before the 1979 Open. I thought, 'Well, I've got second place wrapped up for the Open!' We birdied the last four or five holes, but Seve was miles in front at St Germain.

At The Belfry, Sandy had three good rounds and got into a position to win, but then he thought to himself, 'I don't want to win this week. It might be a bad omen.'

Off we went to St Georges. A couple of years before, when Seve won the PGA Championship there, Sandy's chance of winning went when he lost a ball and two shots after hitting a television cameraman; he felt St Georges owed him something. He played his practice rounds with Bernard, Neil Coles and Tommy Horton. You couldn't get a more unassuming half-past-eight four-ball. But when you get to know them all, and it takes years and years, they're marvellous company. Gallacher and Neil Coles, and then with Tommy Horton after he qualified. We only had about six folks watching us though. We got to the 18th and there's Greg Norman and Jack Nicklaus, who took five hours to get round; we'd done it in less than four, had a bit of lunch and more practice in that time!

Ivor Robson, the starter, was waiting for Sandy every morning, and gave him his usual lecture: 'Listen. You can do it. You can win this. Don't worry about the others.' Good old Ivor. He was peering over the crowd for Sandy every day. Sandy played absolutely fantastically the first two days, but the greens were very strange and unkind to him. His putts wandered off in all directions, so he didn't hole a lot. At St Georges, though, nobody's going to shoot anything spectacular.

Sandy started his tournament with a five. Everybody talks about the five he had at the end and the last hole, but he missed less than a two-foot putt on the first in the first round. He still shot a 68, driving better than he'd ever done before, using a club acquired from Eamonn Darcy only a month before. (It was a driver and it's now mounted in Lyle Towers because after that he couldn't hit a fairway with it!) Sandy thought his 68 was just about the worst he could have got out of the round, driving like that. He missed five putts of around six feet and that one at the first. A 66 would have been fairer.

On the second day the weather was as bad but we didn't get the very worst of it. That first hole haunted Sandy. This time he took a six on it. He skied his tee-shot and didn't hit enough club for his second, went in the front bunker and couldn't get out. Sandy shot a 71, though, and that left him tied for the lead with David Graham, who we played with, of course, for the third round. We had a 3.15 PM start, and we'd only played one hole when the end of the world looked as though it had come and we had to shelter in the R & A tent.

It was a steady round of 73, but Sandy slipped behind. Bernhard Langer really looked as though it could be his year with a 68, and Sandy was three strokes off the lead. Langer and Graham were on 209, O'Meara and Ian Woosnam, who plenty were tipping, were on 212 and then Sandy and Christy on 212 as well. It was anybody's Open, wasn't it? I said to Sandy, 'At least you're going to be playing with Christy tomorrow. It's a good draw.'

In front of us were Tom Kite and Peter Jacobsen. They were in the thick of it as well. Kite was the danger for the start, but he took a six on the 10th. We could see it. He missed the green on the right and needed a good putt even for his six — so that was him gone, we felt. At that 10th, Christy says to Sandy, 'If either of us two can come back in two-under par, we're going to win this. A couple of birdies and we can do it.' Christy was playing unbelievable golf, but nothing would drop for him. I reckon he could easily have shot 64 again in the last round, but he couldn't hole a putt.

Christy's words came back when Sandy was putts for birdie on the 12th and 13th but misses them both. At the 14th he hits into the left-hand rough. It's knee-deep and reedy. Horrible stuff. He has to hack it out sideways, and he's still short of the Suez Canal. It's very windy, of course, so he decides it's a 2-iron to get to the green and he slams it superbly but it misses right, just off the green. It's about 45 feet to putt but he holes it. I think the 15th is the hardest driving hole of the lot into the win, but Sandy hit a fantastic drive, outdriving Christy by 50 or 60 yards. In fact, Christy's hitting a wood for his second shot and it was going way to the left. From the right you have a chance, but from the left, no chance. Christy's caddie's desperately shouting 'fore', but Christy tells him to shut-up because he wants to hit the crowd!

Sandy then hits a 6-iron for his second, which shows you how long his drive was. He had a choice of two shots and he played the most difficult one — the one that would make his ball stop better and hold. He cut it in and holed the putt from about 12 feet. He knew then he'd got a chance of winning.

The 16th, a short hole, was playing very long. It was the downfall of David Graham. He went into the right-hand bunker, the one place you shouldn't go. Sandy came up only on the front of the green but made three. He thought he'd got too much club for his second shot on the 17th, and he didn't hit it all that hard — a 5-iron — so he came up short of the green, after being in the left-hand semi-rough.

As if we didn't have enough to think about, we also had the performance of the streaker, of course. Peter Jacobsen took great delight in tackling him, but we had to wait while it was going on. Sandy was a bit cheesed off because he couldn't see whether it was a man or woman running about with no clothes on. But what a thing to happen so close from home when you're on for winning the Open!

At the 18th Sandy was in the semi-rough again, this time on the right-hand, with the fairway having yet another of St Georges' hog's backs on the way in. It was tough to keep the ball on the fairways. Over the back of the 18th hole is out-of-bounds; you don't want to go in the bunker on the right short of the green where Graham finished up, so Sandy played it left-to-right. He hit what looked like a tremendous shot and the wind should have pushed it back left-to-right, but it didn't. He was coming out of the rough and flying. It hit the green and finished down in the rough with the flag just over a little rise (he was down in Duncan's Hollow). He needed to have two goes at it and in the end made a good five. He thought he'd blown it, I know. But at that time Langer and Graham were bogeying and they had to birdie the last in the finish to force a playoff. I knew that if Sandy won it gave him exemptions in the US the next year, the US Masters, Tournament of Champions, World Series. It won't be just this week, I thought, it's the doors it opens. It meant the US Tour and that meant an attractive career for me as well as him, I hoped. Well it's history that Langer and Graham never made it, although Langer nearly chipped in at the end to force that playoff and give us a few trembles.

The first thing Sandy said when we met up again was, 'Come back to the house.' He had press conferences to do first and all the ceremony. I got two pints of beer. I was thinking, 'I bet nobody has thought of giving him a beer.' I carried them past security guards, R & A officials; it was like Fort Knox. But I got him his beer in the press conference.

After all the formalities were over I followed Sandy back to his home in my car. I was supposed to be going back to my home, but I finished up driving to Lyle Towers with his clubs and the Open trophy. Sandy had to play in the PGA Benevolent Society pro-am the next day at Sunningdale. It was the best thing that could have happened to him — he was out of the way of everybody. There were only about six spectators. After Sandwich it was just as if you'd gone deaf — no spectator noise, only four people watching! He played reasonably well; four or five birdies and we headed back to his home. By the time we got back there was a marquee in the garden. His wife had invited the press and a load of friends such as Faldo, Gallacher, Horton, Queenie (Michael) King and Neil Coles. Queenie made a speech, of course, and he said, 'We've all come today because Sandy Lyle won a competition.' Then, unlike Queenie, he got lost for words.

Ah, St Georges. Nobody knew who was going to win at the end. I don't think anybody ever will there.

# Pete Bender

*Greg Norman — Turnberry 1986*

'Greg had hit his third shot about three feet behind the pin on the 17th green, but he turned to me and said, "You know, Pete, I'm so damned nervous I can't see the hole. You'd better tell me where to hit it and how hard." I said, "No problem." Hardly able to hold the putter, he then knocked it three feet past!'

*Australian Greg Norman may go down in the record-books as the unluckiest player in the major championships. Lady Luck seems to turn against him when the chips are down — and it is certainly the chips that have gone against him. Bob Tway chipped-in out of a bunker to steal the 1986 US PGA Championship from Norman; Larry Mize repeated the chipping in feat, this time from off the fairway, a year later in the US Masters.*

*But it is more than just the lucky shot that has defeated the Great White Shark. He has perished at his own hands at the death. In early 1986 Norman still had those sickening chip-ins to come, but he was already gaining the reputation of being a great player who could not win a major championship — the mantle to be taken on, and shrugged off in time, by Curtis Strange. Two of the reasons for this reputation came at the first two majors of the 1986 season — the US Masters and US Open. Norman led them both and then lost them both. In the Masters he blew his chances by pushing an over-clubbed second shot into the crowd to take a bogey-five on the last hole and lose by a stroke to Jack Nicklaus after leading going into the last round. Then in the US Open, Norman was three strokes clear of the field by twelve holes of the third round, but slipped away to finish no higher than 12th. Fairly or unfairly, rightly or wrongly, Norman was being labelled a 'choker'.*

*After the crushing disappointments of early 1986, Norman was desperate to prove his critics wrong, and the British Open at Turnberry was the only place to do that. His partner on the fairways, caddie Pete Bender, was determined it would not be lack of inspiration or experience from him that would cost the big Australian this major. Experience was something of which Bender had plenty. By the time he and Norman strode out to try to win the 1986 British Open, Bender had been caddying for eighteen years, having picked up his first serious bag when he was 18 years old. Raised in Santa Cruz, California, Pete was not far from Monterey, where the old Bing Crosby tournament used to be held. It was at Monterey where Bender broke into big-time caddying.*

@ @ @

When I got out of high school I wanted to be a caddie, so I got some bags at my local club. A lot of the members told me I was very good — I could pull clubs well and read greens — and I should try going to the Bing Crosby to work for a pro in the tournament. So I did. In the 1968 Bing Crosby I carried Frank Beard's bag. We got on real well and I had a lot of fun that week. The following week the US Tour moved to Los Angeles for the LA Open, and Frank asked me to caddie for him there. That was how I got started. After nine or ten tournaments with Frank I moved on and caddied for Tom Shaw for three years, from 1969 to 1971.

I felt I was working my way up the ladder, and my next player was Jerry Heard, who was a real good player in the 1970s. I was with Jerry for four years — from 1972 to 1975 — and I learned a lot from him. For instance, we didn't have yardage books when I started, and I learned how to use them.

In 1975 I left Jerry and not long after joined up with Lanny Wadkins, who I worked for from 1976 to 1980, when I was ready to move on again. I couldn't move much higher then because I got the opportunity to work for Jack Nicklaus! I was with Jack for nearly two years and during that time I first met Greg Norman. I had my greatest thrill so far, working for Jack in the 1983 US Masters. It was really exciting as Jack finished sixth, shooting a 67 on the last day. That was a highlight for me. We played practice rounds with Greg and for some reason I got talking and joking with him a lot. We got on good together. Suddenly Jack was playing less and less on the tour and so Greg asked me if I'd be interested in working for him. I said I'd have to think about it — playing hard-to-get, you see! Well I did think about it — for about an hour. I called Greg up and said yes, and he said how would I like to start work for him at Muirfield Village? Even though this was Jack's own tournament, I decided to quit Jack after the last event of 1983, the Chrysler Invitation, and start fresh with Greg next year.

At first it looked as though I'd made a big mistake. Jack won his tournament and we missed the cut at Muirfield Village. Afterwards we flew back to Greg's house and we spent the next week working real hard. Then we went back out for the next tournament, the Kemper Open, which we won. After that we never missed a cut together. We really did work well as a team. The big year was 1986, though. We led all four majors and won the Kemper Open again, as well as the Las Vegas Invitational. With the way Greg played that year, he could have done the slam.

The way Greg was playing in 1986, it seemed everything would come his way. But he let the Masters slip out of his hand right at the finish and the doubts must have crept in.

At the US Open at Shinnecock Hills he played the best I'd ever seen him play — probably even better than he was going to in the British Open. We played our practice round with Jack Nicklaus and after it Jack shook his head and said, 'I've never seen a guy play so good. If Greg doesn't win this tournament, then there's something wrong.' Greg was driving superbly, hitting good irons, chipping well and his putting was great. I didn't think we could go wrong. In fact everything was going to plan until the third day when the crowd got to him. He was definitely put off by it all. The rest's history, but he now more than ever wanted to win the British Open.

When we got to Turnberry we found the rough was going to be a major influence on the tournament. It was very high even just off the fairway, and a lot of players complained about it. Greg and I liked it. I believe he's the best driver in the game, and I don't think there's a guy on the US Tour who can drive as far as Greg Norman can. We knew it would be in his favour if he drove well. And if he drove it well, I knew he'd play well. That's exactly what he did all week.

We tried to be real loose before the tournament. I didn't want him to be too uptight or tense, so I kept the jokes coming. As well as the joking, we just went out to enjoy the practice. I'd throw a ball in the bunker and then bet him a Coke he couldn't get up and down. I tried to keep his mind off the real tension before a major championship gets started. We worked the same routine each day for our practice rounds — some relaxed play on the course and some hard work before and after we went out. We played a practice round with Jack Nicklaus, and Jack again told me how well he thought the only threat to Greg might be his confidence.

I wanted a good start and a bit of luck with the weather. I prayed the weather would be on our side; sometimes you can draw the wrong straw with the weather and you're finished. Well, we didn't draw the short-straw but the weather was cold and windy and the course was playing long and tricky. It was tough to make pars and every time we did we were tickled to death. Birdies were definitely hard to come by. We were quite happy to take a 74, four-over-par. That put us in about 15-20th place — quite handy.

@ @ @

*In fact the two-over-par score proved to be more than handy when compared to several of Greg's challengers' cards. The rough had ended the hopes of many an illustrious name: defending champion Sandy Lyle, Tom Watson, who, like Ballesteros had complained about the narrow fairways and deep dune grass fringing them, and Craig Stadler, who shot an 82 and then pulled out of the tournament with a sprained wrist. Stadler blamed the clinging rough for his injury. Another one to fall by the wayside with a 78 was Ray Floyd, who had picked up the US Open title Norman had let slip through his grasp a few weeks before. Practice partner Jack Nicklaus also had an ignominious start, and even Norman himself had contemplated whether he might sue the Royal & Ancient if he injured himself in the dune grass. Greg's first round 74 had not done any damage, though, and he went on to inflict a body-blow on the course, the rest of the field, and the title. The blow came in the form of a 7-under-par 63 for the second round.*

It was a fantastic round, but really, you know, he let it get away from him. He three-putted the last hole for bogey. He had a long putt for a 61 and how he wanted that 61! The round started off pretty slow and we were even after five or six holes. Around the middle he started to string the birdies together and there was no holding him then. It all started to set alight around the 10th and 11th. A big crowd started to gather as Greg got on a real head of steam. I was pumping him up and he responded. I said, 'Come on, there are a lot of birdies left out here still,' and he just kept making them — along with an eagle! The crowd were really worked up by it. I try to caddie aggressively, like he plays. I want him to shoot for every flag. But I didn't have to push too hard that day, everything was going his way, or so it seemed. It was all automatic. Once he gets it going you don't have to do, or say, too much.

It was a shame we finished as we did. Greg hit a good drive at the 18th and then put a 3-iron on the green. He knocked it on to about 35 feet. I tended the flag for him and he wanted that putt so badly. He said to me, 'Pete, I want this one. I want a 61.' But it wasn't to be: he knocked the putt by about 3 feet and then pulled the one coming back wide and finished up shooting a 63. It would be tough to say he was disappointed with his round, but there's no doubt the last hole left a bitter taste in his mouth. We'd played with Ray Floyd who had had a 78 on the first day. He shot a 67 and nobody knew how good that round was because they were all talking about Greg's 63.

We'd had some pretty awful weather already, but the third round was the worst of the week. The day was brutal. I remember trying to hold the umbrella against the rain and the wind was gusting over 40 miles per hour. If I hadn't had the golf-bag on my shoulder, I would have taken off with the umbrella.

We shot another 74 and we were as glad of it as in the first round. We struggled coming in, making four or five bogeys. But they were good bogeys. Greg had said before the tournament that the secret of winning might be in not taking worse than bogey and that definitely applied to the third round. Some of the holes even we couldn't reach in two on the par-4s, they were playing so hard and long. We just kept our heads down and tried not to make mistakes. The most exciting thing about the day was getting off the 18th green. Neither of us could wait to get the round over, we were so cold and miserable. Tommy Nakajima wasn't either of those things. He'd come on strong towards the end of his round to pull up within a shot of us. It was some 71 he scored.

There was a lot of pressure on Greg for the fourth round, and that made his eventual victory even greater. The press and the experts had put the monkey on his back that he couldn't win a major, that he seemed to be 'choking on Sundays'. But we got some of that pressure off right away, and I think it proved very important as far as the way the tournament went from then on.

We had that one-shot lead, and for the par-4 start we hit a 1-iron off the tee because it's a real tight hole. You just have to lay it up. Well we knocked it on and made four but poor old Tommy had a disaster. He three-putted from three feet and made a double-bogey at the very first hole. That helped us a lot. It opened up a three-shot lead going into the second and that gave us a nice little cushion to work with. When we came to the third hole I thought we were going to need some of that cushion. It's a long par-4 and Greg hit his second shot into a greenside bunker some way from the hole still. Tommy was on the green. It was a long, long bunker shot — and into the wind — but Greg hit it great. It took one bounce and rolled right into the hole for birdie. Tommy looked at us and shook his head. He couldn't believe it. At that moment I think he felt it was Greg's day.

This opened up a four-shot lead but at the 5th Greg hit a bad second shot and chipped up, missed the putt and dropped back to three ahead. It worried him a bit, but it wasn't here that he looked nervous and gave me reason to be concerned. That came at the 7th tee. He hit a low, snap duck-hook off the tee, which I have very seldom ever seen him do. Right then I knew something was wrong. With having all those years experience, I know when a player is nervous or choking, whatever people want to call it. His ball had gone into deep rough and I noticed he was walking toward it much faster than usual and he was talking to me faster. I said to myself, 'Oh boy, it's getting to him. He's feeling the pressure.' We've been a bit lucky because, although our ball is in high rough — and I mean high; it was up to Greg's knees — we've caught a good lie, so he can hit a pitching-wedge back on to the fairway. He knocked it on to the fairway, hit his third shot on to the green and then two-putted for par. As we were walking to the next hole I tried to think of the right things to say to him, so I said, 'Greg, do me a favour. You're playing too fast right now. You're real nervous and you need to slow down a little. You're the best player here and you'll win this golf tournament, but you've got to take your time and enjoy it. Don't rush it; don't be nervous. I'm here to help you.'

I don't know whether I got through. He started walking away and he's still walking kind of fast, so I grabbed his sweater from the back and pulled on it to slow him down. I said, 'Whoa! Slow up and walk my pace. Let's have fun. Let's talk and let's just have fun.' I changed the subject and thought of a joke. He started to laugh and joked back. He said, 'Pete, you're absolutely right. I've got this won. Why try and pressurize myself into losing it? Let's have fun.' He seemed relaxed again, and I told him, 'Hit a good shot and just relax.' He did just that.

At the next (8th), a long par-4, he hit a 4-iron second shot about eight feet from the hole. It was a great shot. He made birdie to open up a four-shot lead I looked at him and winked. He looked over and winked back. I knew from there on in he was going to win. He'd settled down.

The 14th tee-shot was the only one to give me concern from then on in. And in the finish it was the hole everyone will probably remember as the one which finally sealed Greg's win. He drove his tee-shot right and into the rough, but he caught a good lie. I think I said it was a 6-iron or maybe a 7, but I gave him the yardage and he hit his shot right at the hole. It was perfect. One bounce; it hit the flag-stick and dropped about three feet from the hole. I remember walking up the fairway and saying to him, 'You're not that good!' He looked at me and hit me on the shoulder. I said, 'Were you aiming at that flag?' He said, 'Of course I was.' Whether he was or wasn't, it was great to have a shot like that at that point. Everyone will remember how good Greg's golf was that week when they think about a shot like that. He made the putt to open up a five-shot lead.

At the 15th he knocked it on to the green comfortably, but we had a long wait because poor old Tommy was in trouble again. He'd hit his ball into the creek and he was taking a drop. We sat down in the grass — in fact I think we stretched out — near the green and Greg said, even then, 'Pete, I'm still nervous.' But this time I think he meant excited-nervous because I think he knew he was going to win his first major.

When we got to the 17th, the last par-5, he hit his third shot about three feet behind the pin, but he turned to me and said, 'You know, Pete, I'm so damned nervous I can't see the hole. You'd better tell me where to hit it and how hard.' I said, 'No problem'.

He knew he had the tournament won, but he was so high he couldn't even line up the putt.

When it was his turn to putt, I told him, 'Inside right lip and soft, on the toe'. When you hit a putt on the toe it kills it. It doesn't go very far and you can't hit very hard. Greg said, 'Okay,' and then he stood over it. He was hardly able to hold the putter. He then knocked it three feet past! So I said, 'Knock it back into the heart of the hole.' He did and made par. Another crisis over.

We went to the last. He wanted to hit driver off the tee, but I said, 'No, no, no. You don't need to hit driver. Hit a 1-iron short of the bunker, then we can probably hit a 4-iron in. Let's not do anything silly like knocking it out-of-bounds.' So he says, 'Okay,' takes a 1-iron and leaves it short of the bunker, and then knocks his second on to the green. That's the last I see of Greg for some time!

The crowd closed in on us. It was pretty hectic — and scary. I got bowled over twice and lost sight of Greg completely, but when I finally got back alongside him at the green he was really excited. I was really happy for him because now he'd answered the question, 'Could he win a major?' Also, he'd silenced all the doubters. He wasn't a choker. He two-putted and we hugged and I told him how proud I was. Then he had to check out his card and his score.

He threw a small private party at the Turnberry Hotel and he invited me. He was in seventh heaven, so excited. I stayed about half-an-hour but I felt I shouldn't be there. I was only the caddie, so I sneaked out.

Greg went out on the course with Laura about 11 PM and sat at the bleachers on the 18th with a bottle of champagne while he went over his round again. He's such a nice guy. Would you believe he took the claret jug Open trophy to a New York jewellers and had an exact copy made up just for me? It's the proudest possession in my house.

# Andy Prodger

*Nick Faldo – Muirfield 1987*

'We really hit it off, and Nick turned round to me and said, "Stick with me, Andy, and I'll make you a millionaire." I said, "Stick with me, Nick, and I'll make you a multi-millionaire."'

Major success for caddie Andy Prodger and Open champion Nick Faldo came the second time around. While they had shared championship success when they had first met, after a split of four years it was their second era together that brought the ultimate honour for them both — the 1987 Open Championship title.

The first part of the Prodger-Faldo relationship yielded the fruits of the two PGA Championship titles of 1980 and 1981. But it was the period between 1986 and 1989 that put Andy and Nick at the fore as the most formidable team in Europe, and probably worldwide, in recent years. As well as the British Open Championship of 1987, there was the Masters title of 1989 at Augusta to make it double major triumphs. And in Europe, Andy and Nick have marched the fairways together to win the 1987 Spanish Open, another PGA title in 1989, the French Opens of 1988 and 1989, and the Dunhill Masters and Volvo Masters of 1989. Andy also had Nick's bag in the English Dunhill Cup win of 1987 and, of course, carried it in 1987 when Europe beat the US in the Muirfield Village Ryder Cup, and in 1989 when the two countries tied at The Belfry. They were also together when Faldo won the 1989 World Matchplay Championship at Wentworth.

Andy has also been successful with other players: he was with the American Tom Purtzer when he won the 1984 Phoenix Open, with Craig Stadler from the US when the 'Walrus' won the 1985 Swiss Open, *and there were two World Cup triumphs for Andy and his man — an individual title with Englishman Howard Clark in the 1985 Cup, and a team title with David Llewellyn of Wales in 1987.*

*For the diminutive Andy — people often wonder how he hauls around the pro bags that stand as high as him — the triumphs he has shared with Nick Faldo are something of a fulfilment of his own ambition of winning the titles himself: he started as a tournament professional with dreams of a major championship before realizing he would not make the grade as a pro, and so took up the bag instead of the club.*

*Born in Edgware, in greater London, in 1952, Andy moved to inner London when he was just two years old. When Andy was fifteen years old he began working during his vacation periods at the local driving range near Bushey in Hertfordshire collecting practice balls. Andy worked hard at his game, and soon landed a job as an assistant to the Hunt family at Hartsbourne Country Club, with Ryder Cup players Bernard and Geoff Hunt and their father 'Pop'. Andy worked mainly in the shop, but also had a chance to play with the Hunts as well as with other famous players of the 1970s such as Doug McLelland, John Garner and Peter Dawson.*

*Using the golfing tips he gleaned from such fine players, Andy soon had his handicap down to two. He was by then an assistant pro in its fullest sense, so he decided to try his hand at playing tournaments. Although he qualified for a few regional events, in fact he was aiming much higher: he wanted a crack at the Open Championship. So in 1973 Andy decided to try and qualify for the Open at Royal Troon — and it was here that an incident occurred that changed his career. He had played the first round, but before he had a chance even to hit a ball in the second he was out of the pre-qualifier, suffering from injuries he had received in a car accident with his caddie. Swallowing hard on the disappointment, Andy spent the next few years taking even more blows on the chin.*

I was playing well, but nothing would go right for me. Tournament after tournament, I'd miss the cut by one or two shots each week. I had enough in the end. It decided me that I wasn't going to be good enough to make the grade. It was a real low part of my life. Around 1978 I quit my job with the Hunts at Hartsbourne, and then started a period of

my life I really try to blank out. I tried everything — engin-
eering, factory work — but I needed a fresh-air life. I even
tried window-cleaning, but that didn't work out even
though I was outside. I still had the golf bug.

In 1980 I got chatting to Stan Francourt, the caddie who
was with me when I had the accident in 1973. They used to
call him 'Stan the Man' at Hartsbourne where he used to do
a bit of spare-time caddying. Stan persuaded me to play
truant and take a two-week holiday to Italy where he was
going to caddie for Craig Defoy. It took two days for us to
get to Rome where the tournament was being played, and
of course I hadn't got a bag. However, I knew at least a
couple of players because I'd caddied for Roger Fidler in the
1977 British Open while I was still an assistant, and I'd also
carried Florentina Melina's bag.

I noticed Nick Faldo was pulling a trolley and it made
me curious. I found out he'd fired his caddie John Moor-
house and then he'd tried a German lad, but he'd only
lasted the practice round! Everyone seemed to be avoiding
Nick. To tell the truth, I think they were all a bit scared of
him. I might have been too if I wasn't so new to the game, I
suppose. I approached him and asked him about caddying
for him, and I was very pleased when he said yes.

Well, we had a good tournament, and I'm not sure who
was most pleased when we finished fourth. Anyway, Nick
was pleased enough to ask me to go to Madrid and caddie
for him. I said I would, but I wouldn't see him for a couple of
days because I had to take a train. Nick said, 'I'll pay your
air-fare and you won't have to worry about long train jour-
neys.' So I flew to Madrid with him.

We didn't do quite so well, but we really hit it off. He
asked me to caddie for him for the rest of the year. What a
year it proved to be: he won the PGA at St Georges, and finished second on the Order of Merit. Nick was so thrilled
with my caddying that he told everyone on television in an
interview that 'Andy Prodger has been great. He's helped
me with my putting particularly.' I'd changed some little

thing — a line-up or stance, can't even remember fully — but Nick was over the moon. We stayed together for two years.

Although we won the PGA again, by the Lancome Trophy later on in the year things weren't at their best. Nick said to me, 'We don't seem to be communicating very well. I need a change. I'm not going to say we won't get back together again, but we need a break from each other.' So we split up towards the end of the season and I then went over to the States. Nick had tried to get his US Tour card that year and we'd played a few times in America. It gave me an appetite for working over there, so after Nick and I split up I decided to try my hand across the Pond.

The first tournament I went to was at Tucson, Arizona, and I became what they call a 'parking-lot caddie'. That doesn't mean I started parking cars; it's what they call a caddie who waits in the club's parking lot for a bag. I didn't have a lot of success doing that, so I decided to chance my arm and go to the players' hotel. I saw this little man who looked familiar: it was Chi Chi Rodriguez and he needed a caddie. I was in luck. Although Chi Chi was forty-six or so, he could still play some, and in the eighteen months I was with him he actually broke two course records on the tour. But he got frustrated because, although he was playing well, he couldn't compete with the younger players. So I went to work for Tom Purtzer, who was thrilled to win the 1984 Phoenix Open in his hometown. I got my first taste of the Masters with Tom. He was in the top three after round one, and that gave me my first taste of a possible major win.

It was a trying time, or it nearly was. They'd not long allowed white caddies at Augusta, and the police weren't used to people like me. I was arrested twice, once for trying to get out of the place, and once for just walking around the course, both times without wearing a badge. My feelings towards the Masters were never great until 1989.

# ANDY PRODGER

*Until 1986 Andy caddied for several players, including Gary Player and Bernhard Langer. He was carrying the American Frank Connor's bag when he was approached by Nick Faldo to join up with him again.*

@ @ @

I caddied on a temporary basis for Nick in Los Angeles and in Kapalua. He asked me to go full-time with him, but I said I was committed to Frank. Well, I came home for the 1986 Turnberry Open expecting to caddie for Mac O'Grady but that didn't materialize, so Nick and I joined up in July 1986.

We didn't do too much until the following year when our first win was the Spanish Open at Las Brisas. Before that we played in America during the same week as the Masters at Hattisburg, Mississippi, Nick had four rounds of 67 and finished second. He vowed there and then he'd never return to a tournament like that; he felt that a man of his stature shouldn't be playing in what was, after all, a second-rate event while the Masters was on. He needn't have worried. He was going to win the British Open, so he'd be at Augusta the next year!

At the Scottish Open the week before Muirfield, Nick brought in coach David Leadbetter to correct a fault. Nick was hitting the ball too low, and David told him to swing under more and finish higher. This seemed to work very well for Nick. Just having David there seemed to give him confidence and Nick showed signs of playing really well.

Next week at the Open Nick was swinging really good. He said to me, 'I just feel it's all coming right just at the right time; something's going to happen this week.' There were definite signs of something in the wind and when I saw who we were drawn with for the first rounds — Nick Price and Ray Floyd — both Nick and I were delighted. I knew we were in for an enjoyable day as soon as I heard Nick Faldo say, 'Have you heard this one, Nick?' They spent the whole round telling each other jokes. Not many people know that

Nick Faldo fancies himself as a comedian and a practical joker. He doesn't give off that kind of air, but get him with a mate and there's no stopping him. He's always playing tricks on people.

We played late on the first day and I went round in the morning spotting the pin positions, trying to get a feel for the course so I could give the right informaton to Nick. We birdied the first couple of holes and we were on top of the world. The joke session helped relax the two Nicks and everybody in the group played well. They seemed to inspire each other. We shot a 68 which was three-under, and that was fine. Rodger Davis and gone crackers and had a 64, but we were well in the hunt.

The good feelings of the first day soon disappeared in the second round though. The weather was pretty foul all week, but it wasn't just the weather. We were in trouble from the start because Nick put his tee-shot into a bunker from the first and he couldn't get his second shot very far. That left him deciding for a long time which club to use for his third shot. He was a good while making his mind up which club to hit. I gave my opinion but, of course, it was a big shot so early in the game. When we got to the green, Ray Floyd says to Nick, 'I thought you were never going to play that shot.' It was a significant remark because it acted like a kick up the behind to Nick. I can't remember Nick's exact words but Ray's comment inspired him more than upset him. He said something like, 'I'll ignore that remark, and the best way to treat it is to play well.'

He was out to make Ray Floyd eat his words and get his own back. He didn't quite because Ray had a 68 to Nick's 69, but our group again played well even though it was another tough day, with wind and rain all day. By the end of it we were just a shot off Paul Azinger's lead. This meant we were playing with Paul in the third round and that was good news for me because Paul's caddie is a good friend of mine, Kevin Woodward. But although we were friends, it was strictly business out there. Nick had got the blinkers on

*Deciding the line: Greg Norman and Pete Bender at Turnberry 1986.*

Above: *A caddie's life! Andy Prodger
plays octopus for Nick Faldo at Muirfield
1987.*

Left: *Andy Prodger deciding the yardage
for Nick Faldo at Muirfield 1987.*

Above: *Arnold Palmer this time making up his own mind on club selection, with caddie Tip just making sure.*

Left: *Drake Oddy and Mark Calcavecchia share the excitement of a birdie, at the last at Troon 1989.*

Above: *Jacky Lee fishing for compliments from Greg Norman. Jacky started off his Open-winning adventures with another great Australian, Peter Thomson.*

Right: *'It definitely breaks left-to-right, boss.' Advice from Albert Fyles to Tom Weiskopf.*

*The British Open's most successful caddying brothers — Albert (left) and Alfie Fyles (right).*

now, so there were no jokes, no idle chit-chat. On with the job. He has tunnel vision when he is doing well.

The weather was lousy again, in fact it was terrible for about three-quarters of the day and it eased off a little when we went out. When I'd checked the pin positions in the morning I'd decided that it was going to be someone already under par who would be in a position to win next day as opposed to someone coming through the field, because I just couldn't see anybody scoring well. Sandy had the best round of the day by scoring a 71 in awful conditions. He never hit more than a 1-iron off the tee.

Paul started badly, bogeying the first. It was one of the few times he didn't get up and down from trouble, and that put us level. But then he started to go well and he got in front again. He seemed to play that first nine better than the back nine every day. He wasn't at ease with the back nine. It was certainly so in the final two rounds, and that was another significant fact in Nick winning. Nick was just as comfortable on the back as the front nine.

There was another significant thing happened on the back nine, as well. On the 13th we were warned for slow play. It was like water off a duck's back to Nick, but I'm sure it upset Paul. Paul just got the edge in the finish, though. He holed a great putt on the last for a five and we both shot 71s because Nick hit a poor second shot on the last and he took a bogey five as well. By Nick bogeying the last it meant he wouldn't be playing in the last group which was now Paul and David Frost. We were paired with Craig Stadler.

It wasn't a very nice day again; this time there was a good old Scotch mist and it was damp and cold. We just kept parring everything, 18 straight pars, as everyone knows. But they weren't just ordinary straightforward pars. Some were real scrambles and gave me hundreds of grey hairs.

Nick got up and down three times from bunkers, at the 7th, 8th and 10th, and they were really crucial. The 8th will live in my mind forever, I don't know whether it does

Nick's. He had a shot out of sand of about 35 to 40 yards into the wind which is probably one of the toughest shots in golf. Nick put it to a yard from the pin. A brilliant shot. I was really elated. I said to him, 'Great shot, Nick,' but he hardly showed any emotion. The blinkers were really on now.

The birdies just would not come, though. We'd had a couple just stay on the lip and we were getting desperate. To make it worse, I think Paul had gone three shots ahead, at eight-under as he again played the first nine well. I had a feeling he'd get edgy after the turn, though.

But we had to do something quick. Nick asked me to read the putts with him but still nothing happened. He was perplexed. He said to me, 'I'm hitting good putts, Andy, but they're not going in. Do you think I'm not supposed to win this?' He must have really thought that at the 9th. We were in between clubs. He wanted to hit a 4-iron but I thought that would never get to the hole. I was searching for birdies and eagles with Azinger going great guns, so not getting there was no good to me. I said, 'Hit a 3-iron. If you get a soft bounce with your 4 you're going to have a very difficult chip. Give it a chance to get there.'

In front of the 9th green there are several ridges and he hit one of these on its down-slope. His ball bounced through the back of the green and he didn't get up and down for a birdie. He blamed me all right, but he didn't say a lot. I knew I was taking some rare old stick mentally, though. He didn't let it affect him for too long, although he put his second into the bunker at the 10th. He got up and down again and this was a real tough hole, 475 yards but still a par-4. Most players were bogeying it on Saturday and Sunday.

We still couldn't get that birdie putt, though. On we went, par after par, until we got to the 16th and I thought, this must be it. It's 188 yards, a short hole, of course, and Nick hit a really great tee-shot to about five or six feet. You could feel the crowd willing it in but it didn't make it and I was beginning to feel it was slipping away, and especially when we could only make par at the 17th. You're always looking for a four on a par-5, but at that stage you'd take it as long as your main opposition hasn't gone away. It was a very brave putt of Nick's to save par, anyway.

As it happened, the way Paul played that 17th he'd have taken par any day. Fortunately for us, and unfortunately for Paul Azinger, he drove into the bunker on the 17th — the one place you must not be. If he could relive that shot I'm sure he'd never take a driver there off the tee (Azinger has said just that in print) because it lost him the Open.

We were just walking off the 18th — with yet another par, and yet another good one but without a birdie to the end — when the crowd started fidgeting because they were looking at the scoreboard. When Paul's score at the 17th came on they were close to erupting, so while Nick signed his card I stood beside the 18th green. I watched Paul play his second and I'm sure he was just like us on the 9th, in between clubs. He made a terrible swing of what I believe was a 4-iron and pulled his ball into the left trap. I'd like to say I walked over to check it out; I didn't run there, but my mind did. I looked at his ball lying there and I thought, 'Well, I know he's been getting up and down from bunkers all week, that's one of his great strengths, but he's going to have to work hard here.' I know it sounds as if I'm being clever, but I felt then we'd won. He darned nearly did it. His bunker-shot wasn't very good, but his follow up putt was. Only a fraction harder and it would have made it.

All this time Nick was in the scorer's hut, watching the action on television. It must have been terrible for him. He was with his wife and baby and I believe he had a cry in there when he knew he'd won. He came out fairly composed, though, before the presentation.

To be frank, I was a bit upset with the way it finished. It was great to win but I was disgusted with the way spectators cheered Paul's bad shots and when he went into the bunker. I spoke to him afterwards and apologized for the crowd, as if it was my fault! He just said, 'Well you can't help it. That's just life.' But the R & A remarked on it during the presentation, about the unsporting behaviour of some sections of the crowd, and it was an unsavoury ending to a great day for me. Another thing that was a disappointment for me was missing the traditional breaking through the ropes and the spectators at the end; getting the police escort through to the last. I hope I've still got it to come. The crowd cheered us in of course, but it's not the same as coming down the last as the winner for sure. Sandy and Dave had it the same. You do regret missing the buzz.

Well, Nick collected the good old claret jug and I stopped to think, 'What does this mean to Andy Prodger?' It meant I was now one of the few. I was now alongside such as Dave Musgrove, Willie Aitchison and Jimmy Dickinson. But I didn't have much time for celebrating it in Scotland. I'd promised my mother I'd buy her some new central-heating, and the only time it could be fitted was the next week, so I needed to be home for Monday when the workmen came round. I might have been able to afford to pay them on the spot because of the win, but I still had to get home on the train that night. My celebration consisted of a few beers with my caddie friends at Edinburgh station and on the night train. Nick stayed at Muirfield for a morning press conference next day and then flew down to play in a charity pro-am. I couldn't caddie for him because I was with the central-heating men.

Looking back on it, I think David Leadbetter's swing change was important. So was the way Nick could relax on his opening two rounds. It was good to do that before the pressure came on. Maybe Ray Floyd stung him into action too. Paul's unease on the back nine was critical, and there were other points: Nick changed his putter at the last minute. But that last round of 18 pars told in the end. The secret of success, in my opinion, is to make pars when you aren't playing well. When you're playing well you make birdies. When the pressure is on you still have to make those pars. Nick Faldo was very successful at that!

# Ian Wright

*Severiano Ballesteros — Royal Lytham & St Annes 1988*

'When I spoke to two of Seve's ex-caddies and asked for advice on how to caddie for him they said, "Don't!" I don't know what made me hit it off with Seve. If I did I'd bottle it and make a fortune!'

Seve Ballesteros is well known for the number of caddies he has been through — Dave Musgrove, Nick de Paul, Peter Coleman and brother Vicente Ballesteros. It was Ian Wright's mastery of yardage charts and his reputation as an accurate reader of courses that first got Seve interested in the caddie. Not only did Ian land what is arguably the most sought-after job in the caddying business, he went on to achieve what is surely the highest aim of any bag man: to bring in the winner of the Open Championship.

Ian Wright is a North Yorkshireman through and through. When he is not carrying Seve Ballesteros' bag — just a few short weeks around Christmas — he is enjoying a beer or playing a round of golf on the links at Cleveland Golf club in his seaside hometown. He is a proficient golfer, playing to eight handicap, which is a great help when accompanying professional golfers around the course.

Born in 1948, Ian first turned to golf after 'getting run out too often playing cricket', but it wasn't until 1983 before he picked up a bag for someone else. A little while after being laid off from his insurance agents job, and some years after leaving his trade work as a radio and television engineer, Ian began a caddying career that has taken him right to the top of his profession.

He is known as 'Two Bags' to his caddying contemporaries because when he first started playing regularly with two local pros, Barry Stevens and Philip Harrison, they both asked him to caddie for them in a

*European Tour tournament pre-qualifier at Leeds. It seemed he had to choose which one, but finished up working for them both — and someone else!*

⊕ ⊕ ⊕

Barry Stevens didn't do any good and as we were finishing, Philip Harrison came into the parking lot, so I asked him if I could caddie for him in the afternoon. He said sure and he qualified, but he'd already arranged for a caddie for the tournament proper, so he fixed me up with Donald Stirling. Donald played all four days and so he was able to pay me what wasn't an astronomical fee. The money wasn't so important, but it was my introduction proper to caddying, especially as I met an experienced caddie, Roy Holland, Brian Waites' caddie, who said he'd help me get settled in if I wanted to take it up as a career.

I went home to my wife and asked her if she'd mind me having a bash at caddying and she said no, so off I went down to Royal St Georges for a tournament at Sandwich. Here I caddied for Graham Burroughs in the PGA Championship, and Graham did well and played all four days. But can you guess who won that 1983 Championship? You've got it — Seve Ballesteros. Anyway, during the Championship I got talking to David Jones in the snack-bar and I found out he'd just parted company with his regular caddie, so I asked him if I could work for him. David took me on for eight tournaments, and the only cut we missed was unfortunately the big one, the pre-qualifier for the Open. He didn't really need a full-time caddie, so David advised me to find someone else, so I arranged to work for Brian Marchbank. It was a most enjoyable time, even though Brian had a lot to put up with. I was relatively new at the job. Still we were fairly successful, and his best finish was fourth at Haggs Castle in the Glasgow Classic. Brian was a gent and very good to me. In fact I couldn't have had a better start than David Jones and Brian Marchbank, they encouraged me tremendously and taught me a lot about caddying.

In my third year I started my yardage book business while at the same time I was freelance caddying. I floated about, getting as much experience with different golfers as I could. I felt if I was going to get to a reasonable level of caddying, I'd have to work with a lot of different people to see how things were done.

I had about thirty golfers buying my yardage books first of all, but by 1986 I had seventy on my books. The yardage books were all hand-drawn. I used to measure the course on a Monday, draw them up straight after and then photocopy them, working all through the night to make them up into books. I wasn't the first, but I don't think anybody had done it on a week-to-week basis. It was very tiring because I was also working for Magnus Persson full-time. I think it was the books that got me known among the pros, and the top pros at that. Nearly every top player that came here for the tour used my books — Greg Norman, Bernhard Langer, Sandy Lyle, and so on. It was nice they had faith in me. Seve was one of the few who didn't take my book, though!

While I was working for Magnus in 1987 I first got wind of Seve being interested in me. I was at Las Brisas when Vicente Fernandez asked me if I'd be interested in working for Ballesteros, Magnus said I ought to take my chance of working for someone like Seve and that he wouldn't stand in my way. Seve said he'd get in touch but he never did, so I forgot about it. I split up from Magnus at the end of 1987 and started working for Carl Mason.

I was caddying for Mase at Puerta de Hierro when two caddies who'd recently come back from the US said they'd heard I was working for Seve this year. I said it was the first I'd heard of it, and that it would be nice if he told me. Well, Seve came into the lounge and asked me if I was working for Carl all year. What could I say? I told him I was committed. But soon after I saw Seve in the locker-room so I took a deep breath and talked to him again about caddying for him. That was when we decided I'd work for him on a four-tournament trial basis, starting with the PGA Championship at Wentworth.

Well, I caddied for Seve at the PGA, French Open and Monte Carlo Open, but after the French he indicated that I didn't have to worry about the trial period. I felt I'd survived the trial when he started talking about other tournaments for the rest of the year. But I'd had a good start. We finished tied second in the PGA Championship, fourteenth for the French and third in Monte Carlo, then we came to the 1988 British Open.

Seve has a tremendous sense of humour if you can bring it out of him — and that stretches to my Yorkshire jokes. It can come in handy to break his thoughts with a joke, to stop him being too intense; it gets him away from thinking about a bad shot he might have played two shots ago and it relaxes him. When he's relaxed between shots he settles down and plays like only Seve can.

On club selection, most of it's confirmation, but if he asks you which club, you have to give the reason why too. On reading putts, he calls me in occasionally. Some weeks he never asks me a line — in the 1988 Open he asked me to read them with him on the last nine holes.

I think we are very good foils to each other. I'm very quiet on the course — even placid. When he wants to vent his feelings I just stand and listen, let him get his frustration out so that then he'll relax and get on with it. I even use the moments when he gets water, fruit or cereal bars on the course as moments for a quiet break from the pressure of the tournament, that's when you need to say things like, 'Keep it going we need a couple of birdies now.'

*Now in his third year with Seve Ballesteros, Ian Wright has found his life changed drastically from his 'two-bag' days. In his first season with Seve*

*they won seven tournaments together, one of them, of course, being the British Open.*

*Although Severiano Ballesteros had let it be known that he was satisfied with his new caddie by talking of tournaments they would do together later on in the year after the Lytham Open, Ian Wright was still serving a four-tournament trial period. The first three tournaments had been safely negotiated, but now came the ultimate test.*

&#9678; &#9678; &#9678;

After the 1988 Monte Carlo Open, in which we'd finished third, Seve went home to prepare for the British Open at Lytham. He just said to me, 'Make sure you're there on Sunday.' I was there all right. Seve decided he wanted to play nine holes, so we threw everything into my car. After we'd registered, we went out to the course. Seve was hoping to avoid the public, but there was no chance of that. Even at this stage there were about 150 people following us for the practice. It certainly gave me the flavour of what it was going to be all about, and I think gave us a proper feel for the course. I'd already done my yardages on the course, so I was prepared. We played a few holes of the first nine and then cut across to do a few of the back nine.

The next day we worked out our strategy for each hole. We usually make a plan for each hole and how we are going to play it, and then vary it according to weather conditions if necessary. We normally stick to the plan if the conditions are reasonable

I met Seve at 5.30 AM for the practice round. He told me literally exactly how we were going to play hole by hole, and I made all the necessary notes, checked the yardages, distances, and also more particular matters — like distances to bunkers and other crucial parts of the course. We played with Sandy Lyle and Nick Faldo, and the crowds following us were just phenomenal. Right from the start people seemed to be encouraging Seve; they were right behind him even then.

On Tuesday we played a four-ball. Wednesday we didn't intend playing at all, just practising, but Seve decided at the last minute to go out for nine — and weren't the crowds pleased about that! We then practised chipping and putting, fine-tuning everything. Seve spent a lot of time on the putting green on Wednesday — he spends an hour every day on his putting, anyway.

Thursday — the big day. Our tee-off time was about 9.25 AM, and so I'd be meeting Seve at least an hour-and-a-half before that. Sure enough, he arrives about eight. We got the gear sorted out and went straight to the practice area. Putting got the most attention again. Then we were off. I'd waited a long time for the chance of an Open. Here we go!

We started birdie, birdie, birdie, and I'm feeling as if I'm in a dream. We've gone to two shots clear of the field after three holes. Seve took the course apart on those first nine holes. After the daze of the first three, I started to settle down a bit. I got my feet on the ground and started working.

We found our first real trouble at the 14th. The drive was a little off-line and the ball settled on an awkward ridge in the semi, and with it lying a bit awkward, he pulled it left. The club caught the grass and turned it. The ball shot straight left into some pretty wicked jungle — heather trees, gorse and god knows what. We were very lucky to even find the ball and to locate where the green was, which direction it was, how far away, and so on. Then we had to decide where we were going to take the penalty drop because the ball really was unplayable. At this stage there must have been 300 people milling around. I'm trying to charge my way backward and forward through the crowd with the bag on my shoulder. What a mess!

We decided the only sensible way we can play it is to take the ball back towards one of the 6th tees where at least there was a fairway-type grass. I then have to work out the yardage to the green, so go off pacing right up and outside the trees. After some discussion we decide it's a 7-iron. Seve then plays the most magnificent shot over the trees and scrub. He couldn't see where he was going or how far, but we soon found out. It landed about five yards from the pin. He then sank the putt for one of the greatest fives I've ever seen. The putt made it. It felt like a birdie. It wasn't that Seve was one of the few players in the world who could've played that shot, but proof of how he thinks everything out so carefully — the whole thing took 25 minutes — like not trying to hack his way out of impossible situations. It was real elephant-and-tiger country, and then to sink the putt, which wasn't easy because the ball lay on a ridge. We both had a little smile to each other at that point. It was a real bonus to make that save and kept us in good heart, although we had a few anxious moments before coming in two shots ahead of the field.

I was absolutely certain Seve was going to win. I'd never seen him hitting his long irons so well, and good iron play at Lytham is crucial. The putting, everything. There was just something about him — and I'd seen it in the build-up — that gave me a hunch he was going to win. I was full of confidence for the second round, and we started quite nicely, although nothing like the day before, then at the third we brought the bunker into play. I got a ticking off because the one thing we'd planned especially was to keep the ball out of sand. It was the key to Lytham. The bunkers were quite deep, and most of the time there was no chance of getting on for two if you were in them. We had a steady round, though, and at the end of the day we were second, a shot behind Nick Price.

The third day got washed out completely. When I woke up I knew the tournament was going to be in trouble, It had been bad enough when I walked it before play, 18 holes in the pouring rain, but during the morning it started to lie on the greens and some of the fairways. It was a long, boring, tedious day sitting around waiting for something to happen, and it never did. It's very difficult when you're in the middle of a tournament.

For the Sunday third round we started with a couple of birdie chances, but both went begging and then at the 6th we hit trouble. Seve pulled the ball left off the tee, but it didn't look too bad, then we found it had hit a spectator and disappeared into some bushes left of the fairway just behind the ropes. Seve decided the ball had to be played, and opted to hit his shot backhanded to get it out, but on his first attempt it moved no more than about eighteen inches. He decided to play it again and he gets it out on to the fairway this time and makes a six. He kept pretty calm and settled down to play some good golf, getting his round back to one-under-par 70. This was two strokes off Nick Price's lead, and nicely in contention.

The 6th could have been a major disaster. If the second backhanded shot had stayed in we could have taken an eight or worse. Seve's attitude was typical of how he was all week — he didn't let it upset him; he always felt he was in control. He's the man who's got to decide the shot and whether a backhander is right or wrong. He had a chirp at me for being too close and he was absolutely right; his ball could've ricocheted off a branch or root and the last thing we wanted was penalty points, but he could see me out of the corner of his eye. He wasn't as ferocious with me as he's been. I'm not one for saying that one shot changes a tournament, but I think saving shots is crucial.

Monday dawned and it was a strange feeling. I'd had a good night's sleep despite all the thoughts of what the last round meant, but now I had to get my clothes and stuff packed for going home. I didn't change my routine because we had an extra day, though, and I did all my preparation as usual. I still felt we were going to win. We practised one hour before the off, chipping and plenty more putting. We had a light lunch and then we were heading for the first tee. What followed was the most spectacular round of golf I've been privileged to witness.

At first it looked as though it was going to be a battle between six or seven players, but as it turned out it became a battle between two. Everyone seemed to be taking the front nine to bits. There were eagles and birdies flying in all directions. Fred Couples came into the reckoning, Nick Faldo, Sandy Lyle, they were all there. We were aware of the others bunching up and Seve had a couple of reasonable chances of birdies but missed them. He kept calm though and the most he said was, 'I thought that was going to break', or 'I thought there was more swing on that.' He didn't panic. Then all of a sudden we got going. Everybody had been having their charge earlier. Now it was our turn — birdies and an eagle for Nick Price and Seve on the 7th, and by then it became clear we were starting to pull away from the field. By the finish of the 11th it was a two-horse race. Seve was still incredibly relaxed. For a major championship I expected him to be more pumped up, but he kept his head and a very calm manner.

We went one ahead and then I got into trouble. At the short 12th (par-3, 198 yards), I gave him the wrong club and he didn't hit the best of shots. Then, unfortunately, he dropped a shot and that put us back into a tie. He'd hit a 4-iron and certainly it should have been a three, using the left-to-right wind. He normally hits a low left-to-right shot and the green ran that way. Black mark to Wright!

If it had been a special round, from then on it became extra-special. Nick Price hit his ball to inches on the 13th; Seve hit his to about eight feet and holed the putt — still tied. Both dropped shots at the 14th. Nick especially looked as though the putting was getting to him. I felt it could be the chink in his armour. He'd said he'd not putted especially well all week; he didn't look that confident, and I was waiting for the moment where he might crack. Well, it wasn't so much Nick cracking as Seve getting a breakthrough, which came at the 16th when he hit his second shot to inches: Nick two-putted for a four. Back to one up for us. We decided on a wedge for the shot after some discussion whether to use a 9-iron (in 1979 he'd hit a 9-iron from about the same distance when he came out of the parking lot).

I thought Nick Price was extremely lucky to stay in it at the 17th: he hit a fade off the tee, but it hit the fence or something and avoided going into the practice area. He then hit a very good 1-iron into the green, while Seve hit a nice shot to the heart of the green, both parring.

The 18th tee was a real heart-stopping moment for me. Seve drove down the right and I wasn't convinced it had avoided the bunkers. Seve said anxiously, 'Is it past the bunkers?' I told him I was sure it had, although I wasn't sure. It made it a long walk down, and all the while Seve kept saying, 'Are you sure it's past the bunkers?' I kept saying yes, but my heart was in my mouth. At last I saw somebody stood by the ball and only then did I know we were safe.

The plan was to play to the left part of the green with the second because the wind was coming over the top of the stand left-to-right and we knew it was important to keep left. It takes out all the trouble on the right, such as the bunkers. The green slopes left to right, too, I thought we had a bit of what could be a flying lie, and it was also a case of judging just how much adrenalin Seve might have flowing. We decided on a 6-iron. He hit what looked a real good shot, but from where we were standing we couldn't see the ball finish because of a hill on the left of the green. I thought it would have swung left-to-right and finished somewhere just past the flag. When we got to the green it had run off down into a hollow and was nestled in the rough on a down-facing slope. I said to myself, 'This isn't good. We need to get up and down for two to make sure of winning and this isn't an easy shot.'

Seve then produced a magical shot under pressure; it was perfect weight and everything and he nearly holed it. Even now when I watch it on video I think it's going to catch the hole and drop in. Once that happened I felt great and I just knew there was no way Nick was going to hole his putt, which was a long one. He just never had a chance. He knew he had to hit it hard to get into the hole, but it never looked like going in and it went eight feet past. He missed the one coming back, which was sad for Nick. He'd put up one of the greatest performances. He played a great round of golf and he'd done everything he could. I mean a 69 and he'd lost the Championship. He must have felt sick. Seve's 65 was one of the most spectacular rounds of golf to win an Open.

Everything after is a bit of a blur. I remember shaking hands with Andy Prodger, Nick Faldo's caddie, and the next thing Seve and I were hugging each other in the middle of the green and tears were filling my eyes. I remember handing Seve the card and he handed me his club and the ball. I put the club away and shoved the ball into my pocket; nobody was getting them. I'd promised a policeman my overalls for charity so he got them. Then I was grabbed by a radio station sports reporter and I went straight on the air. I haven't a clue what I said to this day. Australian television wanted an interview and then somebody threw down a bottle of champagne from the stand. I fought my way to the exit and the press were there waiting. They wanted me to say a few things but I can't even remember the questions, let alone my answers. One of the guys who'd bet on Seve supplied the champagne, but it took me twenty-five minutes to get to the locker-room where I might have chance to drink it.

It was really strange in the locker-room. With it being an extra day, most of the players and caddies had shot off to get to their next tournament. Only Andy Prodger, Dave McNeil, Nick Price's caddie and another caddie called 'the Judge', were there. While we sat there Nick Price walks in. What can you say to him at this point? I just said I'd really appreciate it if he'd have a glass of champagne, 'for the way you played against us today'. Nick said he certainly would, which showed the character of Nick Price. He must have been feeling terrible, but he joined in the celebrations.

I never saw much of Seve. He went to talk to the press and then on to the presentation, which I watched through the window of the locker-room. An hour after I get a message: 'Can you bring my gear to the car?' Seve said, 'Thank you very much. See you next Tuesday.' It's hard for me to remember where we were next Tuesday!

As I came away from the course a guy from television asked me if I'd like to do a breakfast show. I could feel my whole life was changing. I said yes, not realizing I'd have to be up at 4 AM. I left Lytham at 9.30 PM and got home just after midnight. I did the television show and the next day the phone never stopped ringing, every newspaper I'd ever heard of, and loads I hadn't rang — forty-one different papers! The local television station filmed me at my golf club. I couldn't believe the amount of interest there was in me. I could understand them wanting to know about Seve, but not about me. He was the shot-maker, the one who deserved the credit. I just happened to be in the right place at the right time.

# Drake Oddy

*Mark Calcavecchia — Royal Troon 1989*

'As Wayne was getting set up for his putt, Mark said, "If he makes this, how many putts do I have to win?" I said, "If he makes it you've got two. If he misses you've got three." Wayne missed, Mark said, "I got three from here? That I think I can hit."'

N ever has the saying that a player and his caddie are a team been more in evidence than with bag-man Drake Oddy, whose grandparents emigrated to America from England, and Mark Calcavecchia, the 1989 British Open champion.

The Oddy/Calcavecchia partnership began in 1979 at Gainesville University, Florida. Drake had been there a couple of years when Mark started playing on the golf team. Mark then left to turn pro while Drake stayed on to get a degree. Drake was a good golfer himself, and at one time thought of trying out for the team, but the coach wasn't keen on people going to class.

Drake started caddying for Calcavecchia part-time in 1982, and in 1986 went full-time. Mark didn't want to travel to the US Tour tournaments by himself, so he asked Drake to go along. Two months later he won his first tournament, the Southwest Classic in Abilene, Texas. The two friends added further US Tour victories in 1987 and 1988, the year Calcavecchia so nearly won the US Masters, denied by Sandy Lyle at the death to finish runner-up. By the time they began their assault on the British Open title at Troon in 1989 Calcavecchia had become one of America's hottest golfing properties. Victories earlier in the year in the Phoenix and Los Angeles Opens had put the man from Nebraska to number two on the US money list. Next to two-time US Open champion Curtis Strange and money-list leader Tom Kite, Calcavecchia — and his

*friend from his salad days — represented America's best hope of winning*
*back the British Open title last won for the US by Tom Watson in 1983.*

@ @ @

Mark came over to England a week early because a couple of times in the past (they had played the British Open of 1987 at Muirfield and the previous year at Royal Lytham) we didn't get there until the Tuesday morning. Even by Thursday Mark hadn't felt properly acclimatized. We gave ourselves time this year, and that really helped. We were sharing a room at the Caledonia Hotel, and we had the staff there on standby because Mark's wife was expecting and we didn't know from day to day whether we'd be hopping on a plane back to Phoenix. We had the air schedules worked out for any time of day for us to get back in a hurry.

Mark was in a hurry to get to the course on the Monday though. He picked me up at the airport, we dropped my suitcase off at the hotel and then it was off to the course. It was vital because British courses are so different to American. When we play in the States the only practice round we have is in the pro-am. Mark's not a mechanical player, and he doesn't get much out of just playing and hitting. At places like Troon and Muirfield you have to play at least a couple of times from different parts of the fairways to have an idea of what they're about.

I'd read books on Troon but I never expected it to be so brown and dry. After the first practice round though, Mark's impression was that he liked it. He hadn't liked Lytham the year before. He was never comfortable with it. Rounds of 76 and 84 bore that out! His good shots there didn't get good results, and his bad shots got really awful results. This was different. Sometimes you just have a feeling. Mark felt he'd have more birdie chances here because he hits more greens than he used to, but you have to hit a lot of different shots, and on some holes you couldn't really go for the green. He felt he'd have an advantage around the

Troon greens because he'd developed real good hands. That week he just happened to have an incredible touch around the greens, so his assessment in practice was right.

On Tuesday I did the yardages, and then we played our next practice round with Curtis Strange, Mark O'Meara and Arnold Palmer. We played a match and that was just what was needed. It was relaxing and good for Mark, especially playing with Arnold. We talked with him about the last time he had won at Troon and about the way things were then, what the weather conditions were like, and where he hit the ball on certain holes. Remarkably, conditions had been very similar to what we were experiencing. Arnold had his old caddie Tip and it was wonderful to hark back. It all helped get the feel of Troon. We also played with Mark O'Meara, and we won money off Arnold and Curtis; we took pleasure in taking their money off them and didn't think so much about the coming tournament.

There was a lot we did take in while practising properly, though. The 6th (577 yards, par-5) and longest hole was playing real short, and even the 8th, the Postage Stamp, seemed very benign. There was no wind and the wind provides 70 percent of the difficulty; it's an important factor. On the Tuesday in practice Mark tried to hit a couple of 1-irons at the 17th (223 yards, par-3) but he could hardly get to the green and he had to make sure with a 3-wood. It never played that long during the tournament, and the most he hit for the week was a 1-iron when it was windy. The rest of the time it was 2-iron, 3-iron and even 4-iron. The toughest conditions during the week were Tuesday, and at least when the wind did blow it was in the same way the practice round. At Lytham the year before it blew one way in practice and another in the tournament. That made the holes entirely different.

On the first day proper we had a steady round, nothing spectacular, scoring a 71. The year before Mark hadn't had any fun and he'd vowed that 'No matter what happens, we're going to have a good time.' We were pretty relaxed. We'd played pool the night before and we didn't have to start too early or too late as had happened a couple of times. A 3 PM start for Mark is hard because he's an early riser.

We didn't have too many problems and finished 1 under par. Mark watched some of the guys burning up the course. There's always some guy who gets away in the first round; this time it was Wayne Stephens with a 66. But big tournaments aren't won in one round. The first round you're trying to play well but you just try to get into a decent position. You've come all that way so you don't want to start out poorly and have to grind them out to get back, but we felt we were well in touch.

I don't think Mark played as well in the second round even though he scored well with a 68. He made what we could call some stupid bogeys, for instance where you miss the green on the wrong side of the pin. Most courses you can miss either side of the hole, but at Troon that's not the case. At the first par-3 for example, the 5th (210 yards), if the pin is left, you can't miss left because there's nothing to hit off. When the pin is at the front, there's a big bunker right at the front so he'd said, 'The one thing I mustn't be is short'. That par-3 5th summed up Mark's week because, despite saying that, one day he hit into that bunker, leaving himself a 60-foot shot out of sand. He hit it to six feet and made the putt. So that week, even on the holes where he did what he said he shouldn't do, he got away with it. In the second round, he didn't get away with it a couple of times, or it may have been better than the 68.

There was no wind whatsoever on the third day, something we had made allowance for in practice. Any course where you can shoot straight at the pin is to Mark's advantage. But the thing that worried him in practice was that when we played the first (362 yards, par-4), he hit a ball pin-high and it wound up 40 feet away at the back of the green. He'd said, 'We might have to change a couple of things this week. Luckily they put enough water on the greens so that when there was no wind it was like any other day. This was good because Mark's game is not the bump-and-run. With no wind, you could get to within 20 or 30 yards of the green at the first.

Without a breath of wind on the Saturday, the par-5s were playing exceptionally easily, so we had to take advantage of those and he did. It helped him shoot another 68. It was another unspectacular round really. The fireworks didn't start to go off until the last nine holes of day four.

Going into the last day he knew he had a chance to win. He made a couple of birdies but then three-putted the 7th from about 18 feet. At that point he got somewhat discouraged because Wayne Grady had gotten off to a good start. Once you get to the back nine on a tournament's last day and you're not three or four shots off the lead, there's not much you're going to do about it. These are not bad players; they're not just going to lie down. We were beginning to wonder.

But then things started to happen. The true key to the tournament as far as we saw it, turned at the 11th (481 yards, par-5). Mark's drive went into the overgrowth to the right. He then tried to hit out on to the fairway, but the ground was so hard it just bounced and rolled and rolled — under one of the thorny bushes on the left. He only hit it about 60 yards. Mark was very discouraged, and he hit the ball on to the green to all of 50 feet still. He then ran in the 50-footer and made it for par. At that point he said, 'At least something good's happening today.' There was much more to come.

The 12th was just unbelievable. His second had gone into real rough stuff, and his chip out was going to go 20 or 30 feet by the hole. That green was as hard as a rock but the shot he tried to hit was the only shot he had to play. He just hoped to get lucky. He did: he hit the pin full-on and it dived in the hole. He hit it with a Ping sand-wedge called an L-wedge, and that's what that club's made for. You can hit it high and hit it soft. At that point I think he was four

133

behind — on 11-under to Wayne's 15-under. We looked at the scoreboard and knew that the rest of the holes were playing downwind. He figured if he could make two or three birdies he could move up because no one else was playing all that well by now — except Greg Norman, that is. When we were at 12 Norman was on 13, and at that point we really couldn't worry too much about Wayne because if we didn't catch Greg it wouldn't matter.

At 13 we left it short at about 20 feet and made no impression, and at 14 we were short as well, but here we were in the bunker (180 yards, par-3). Then I knew Mark had confidence because he was lining it up as if it was a putt, looking at the line, how it might roll in the hole. It nearly did roll in; it just lipped out but at that point I knew he was back in the groove, that he felt confident and wasn't just trying to get through or just go through the motions.

When we played 16, he finally got his drive on the fairway after missing it all week. He could have layed up a 3-wood because he was on a bare patch. He said, 'I'm not sure I can even get off this,' and then decided on a driver, which I agreed with. One reason we get along is because we think the same way. We always play an aggressive game. Our theory is always get as close to your objective as possible. Don't worry about what the shot's going to be like around the green, don't worry if it's in a bunker. It's still going to be an easier shot from 10 or 12 yards then it is from 100 yards.'

At that point, though, there wasn't really any other choice for him. He was still three shots behind the lead and this is the last hole you can think about as a birdie chance. He hit the shot unbelievably to 30 feet, and his putt really didn't miss by much for eagle. He was glad of the birdie, though. He knew every one he made now would take him closer to the lead.

At the 17th he hit a 3-iron tee-shot with the pin tucked around to the right. You couldn't really go for the pin. The green was real hard and his ball ran out towards the back left edge to about 40 feet. The putt broke six inches more to the right than we thought. But it turned out to be in our favour in the end. It was exactly where it went in the playoff. He missed both times, leaving it over the edge, but it was a much easier putt in the playoff.

By the time we got up on the 18th tee, Norman was done. We knew what we had to do, therefore. Make birdie. The hole was playing short (425 yards, par-4) and Mark's drive ran through a very hard fairway only a few yards from the bunker Greg was to go in for the playoff. If Mark had hit straighter he would have been in the bunker. His drive had gone about 325 yards, so he only needed an 8-iron and he had a good lie. The weather had resulted in the rough not being so high.

Now people always talk about his 5-iron in the playoff here, but that was a much easier shot to hit when you think out it. He knew he *had* to make birdie this time. He hit it to about 10 feet, it took one hop and sort of juiced back to the right about four feet. With out-of-bounds being only 20 feet past the pin, it was a fantastic shot. It was a perfectly straight putt, but I'm not sure if it had any break he would have played for break anyway. We think if it's only got a little break the best thing to do is hit it a little firmer and straighter. Then you don't have to worry about the break. That's what he did. We were tied with Greg.

It wasn't until we got off the 18th green that we knew Wayne had made bogey on 17. Then when we saw his ball go over the 18th green we knew it would be hard for him to birdie. We were in a playoff in 20 minutes time. Mark went straight off to chat to an ABC interviewer. Suddenly I realized I might not have enough golf balls. I had just three new balls left and the playoff was over four holes. You never know what can happen. We normally go through 12 or 13 balls a round on average because Titleist are so soft. Luckily Tom Watson had plenty. He'd come off the last with Wayne after a great bid to win the tournament himself. He left us half-a-dozen balls. As it turned out we only needed our three. We still had 15 minutes before the restart, so we just sat around the putting green with Greg and Wayne. It was all pretty friendly. They've played a lot of golf together.

The four-hole playoff was more relaxing. There wasn't so much tension on the first tee knowing that it wasn't a case of bogey you're out, birdie you win. Mark was wary and still surprised it was four holes. He kept asking the R & A guys, even on the tee, 'You're sure now? I mean, it's four holes, right? After one hole nothing changes, right?' It was a good job it was. Greg made birdie on the first (1st, 362 yards), of course. Mark made a six-footer for par. He didn't want to be two down right at the start.

At the second playoff hole (2nd, 391 yards) Mark hit a good drive but the second shot to the green bounced over into the back fringe. It was a good shot, but the green was so firm. Sometimes when we line-up putts Mark has a feeling, sometimes he doesn't. Sometimes he can picture a line better than other times. Sometimes he says, 'This is in.' I would say he only does that 10 or 12 times a year. Eighty percent of the time it goes in, and I mean putts of 30 or 40 feet, which is what this one was. As he went over the putt he said to me, 'This one's in, I know.' It went right in the middle of the hole. But Greg got his from about 10 or 12 feet. At least we were keeping within range.

On 17 we hit the same shot as earlier on. Greg hit first and in the air it was right at the pin but it finished over the back edge. Wayne hit his into the bunker. We were surprised when Greg decided to chip instead of putt. There didn't seem that much between him and the green that would cause him trouble, but you can only go with what you feel at the time. He ran it by the hole but he could still make the putt. But this time it was to save par. We played with David Feherty in the last round and he had the same putt and missed it. There was a good four-inch swing to the right on it. We knew Greg would have to read something it it David didn't see. He couldn't and we were level. Wayne had parred the first two holes and he bogeyed here, so we thought it was really Mark versus Greg.

I'd thought I'd have to be calming Mark down by now but I was amazed to see how cool he was. Here we have the biggest tournament in the world, seen by the most people in the world, and he looked pretty cool. Some players work better being excited. Four or five birdies in a row and the gallery's going crazy, even his wife is hopping about, but Mark feels the next hole is just important as the previous one. That's what amazed me about the playoff. We had a laugh about something after we'd putted out on the 17th green. He'd be able to tell you what we were laughing about better than me, because I was so nervous I don't remember what it was about! But I try to have a laugh like that most of the time. I try to get his mind off it when we're not actually playing. You have to have some kind of outlet.

At the 18th he hit an awful drive. It wasn't totally out of control but it was really going right. It hit some of the cameramen around the edge and came back. If there were no photographers and no gallery, it would have been 25 yards right of the fairway where the rough would have been just that bit higher. But you don't want to hit left. There's a series of bunkers and if you get in those you can't get to the green. One day in practice we hit left of those bunkers and it was the only place where the grass was high. Left was no place to be, especially hitting first. You don't want to make it easy for the other guy. I don't think it was matter of him letting up on the swing on the tee, just that he spun out more than normal.

Then Greg hit his into the bunker. Wayne was safe. We had a good lie. But before we hit our second, we both walked up to look at Greg's lie. We had to see the situation. At this point, Mark and Greg could make bogey and Wayne birdi, so it could finish a tie. It was like matchplay. We didn't think there was any way Greg would try to go for the green. It wasn't just because he was bunkered. The bunker face was hard-packed. If you were to catch any part of it you were more likely to hit yourself than the green. We felt the very best Greg could do was a four.

We had 205 yards to the pin. We decided on a 5-iron. All Mark was trying to do was land it on the front part of the green and let it roll. It took off and it never, ever wavered. It didn't fade an inch; it didn't draw an inch. He could have hit a hard six but that may not have done the job and he could have finished short, or even worse, in one of the bunkers. When it was in the air he said, 'It doesn't matter where the ball goes. I don't have any better than that.' If, while it was in mid-air, someone had said to him, 'Do you want to try that one again?' Mark would have told them, 'I'll take that one.' We knew it was inside 10 feet and so did Greg. He knew Mark had a good chance of birdie so he had to go for the green. He was unlucky that it trickled back into the bunker. Once he was in there it was a hard shot. We walked up to the green and saw Mark's putt was about six or seven feet but it wasn't quite the same as knowing you had a two- or three-shot lead. We still had some work to do. If we'd known Greg was then going to hit out-of-bounds it would have been a lot easier.

It's a great stadium feeling at the last in the British Open. You have different people in the crowd rooting for different players, but they all appreciate good golf.

There was great confusion after Greg hit his third shot out-of-bounds — Wayne was on the green — because he was told by a man from the R & A he must hit another shot. Greg just said, 'Go ahead. I'm done. If you happen to four-putt I'll go back and hit another one.' Mark just wanted to know where he stood. He didn't want to get in a position where he thought his opponent had taken a certain number of strokes and he hadn't. That's part of my job — to keep track of where he is and where everybody else is.

At that point with Greg having blown out, Wayne was in with a chance for birdie. He'd hit a great second shot from the fairway which came close to going in, which would have meant Mark needing a birdie to win. As Wayne was getting set up for his putt, Mark said, 'If he makes this, how many putts do I have to win?' I said, 'If he makes it you've got two. If he misses, you've got three.' When Wayne misses Mark said, 'I got three from here? That I think I can hit.' He lined up the putt and I said, 'What are you lining-up for?' He said, 'It would be nice to make it.' But then as he walked towards it his only thought was, 'Don't double-hit the ball.' He told he he thought to himself, 'What can possibly go wrong?' The only thing he could think of was if he hit the ball twice. He hit a great putt and that was the only way to win. It was better than dribbling it up or lipping out. It would have been great to have made that putt if the competition was close. But it was a win. Afterwards it was hard to appreciate it all — birdie finish or whatever. It was later when we felt the joy of it.

We talked to friends back home and they were going crazy. We'd liked to have been with them. A good few of the American players had stayed on — some even came back from their hotels to congratulate Mark. But as happy as he was, and as worried about his wife, who was about to go into labour, he still had time to think about his mom and dad because they'd sacrificed so much for him to be able to play golf. His father had died the year before Mark won his first tournament, and he stopped to think just how his dad would have felt, as he held on to the British Open trophy.

# Almost there . . .

## Peter Coleman

'I've got to the top of the caddying tree carrying the bags for the likes of Seve, Greg and Bernhard, but it was a woman who gave me my first big break — Nancy Lopez. Peter Allis called me the kissing caddie because every time Nancy sank a putt she'd give me a big smackeroo . . . and she sank a lot of putts!'

No book on caddies could possibly be complete without a few words from Peter Coleman, arguably the most successful caddie of this era, whose players have won no less than thirty-six top titles on either side of the Atlantic — and the other side of the Pacific, in Australia. Peter has yet to feel the exhilaration of walking down the 18th fairway as his player receives the accolade reserved for an Open champion, but he has not given up hope yet.

Peter Coleman was the first British caddie to accompany a US Masters winner, and, in the latter years, the Coleman image has elevated the bag handler to a higher status. He can rightly say he has been a pioneer — he was also the first caddie to win sponsorship endorsements — with the bag after introducing 'the wheel' to European tournaments to measure yardages. With his perm and his Porsche, Coleman became the first caddie celebrity as he went from the bags of Tommy Horton, Seve Ballesteros (twice), Greg Norman, and his present boss Bernhard Langer, the player with whom he shared the triumph of Augusta.

Peter Coleman came from a poor family. To earn pocket-money he would caddie at weekends over the course at Coombe Hill near New Malden in Surrey when he was only eight years old. When he left school at fifteen he found a job in a surveyor's office, but soon left because he could *not bear being indoors. He decided to get out of the office, take a few odd-jobs, and concentrate on his golf handicap.*

*Within two years he was down to two handicap, and that earned him a job as assistant to George Howard at New Malden. The year was 1956. Peter lasted only eighteen months, for as an assistant, he was earning a tiny amount that was not enough to keep himself, let alone to contribute into his poor family's home.*

*After a succession of jobs Peter began the 1970s working for British Rail, where he stayed for four years or so until he started to get itchy feet again; the call of the fairways was too strong for a man who was used to being footloose and fancy free.*

@ @ @

My first professional bag of any repute was for Tommy Horton at Finham Park, Coventry around 1974 for the Piccadilly tournament.

While I was with British Rail I learned a lot about measuring and I had my own measuring wheel. I used to walk the course with it before each tournament and, even in those days, my yardages were 100 percent accurate. The other caddies used to laugh at me, but they soon stopped laughing when Tommy started winning tournaments and saying it was because of my accurate yardages. In the end the caddies were coming to me to check yardages. It took a lot of hard work, but I thought if I'm going to do this as a career I'm going to do it properly.

I think yardages are the most important function of a caddie. After that comes reading the greens, and then it's essential you never worry a player by being late for anything. Also, you must keep yourself clean and tidy — then let your actions do the talking.

Spot-marking next to or on the fairways makes working out the yardages much easier nowadays. I used to spend more than a day measuring from bunkers and trees to the greens. Tommy was quiet and easy-going but with Seve you couldn't afford to make any mistakes. And you couldn't go off 30 or 40 yards pacing-out in those days with

Seve. It always meant a lot of work before I even met up with my player. Even before a pro-am I'd be up at 5AM measuring up.

I worked for Tommy for about four years, and in between carrying his bag I carried for Nancy Lopez when she came over to play in Britain. She was just a young girl, and her first tournament in Britain was also only her second as a professional. She came second behind Judy Rankin at Sunningdale. We got quite a bit of coverage on television because every time Nancy sank a putt she gave me a smackeroo on the cheek — and she sank a lot of putts! Peter Alliss nicknamed me the 'kissing caddie'.

I don't think it was the kisses, but Nancy asked me to go back to the US with her and caddie there. I didn't think I was ready, and I wasn't sure I wanted to travel that far so I said no. She really made an impact on the golfing world soon after and I think I regretted my decision. But that was my big break, and it was the start of my being recognised as a top caddie. It was also the start of a new image for the caddie in general, I suppose. Before then it had been just a job, but the old-style caddie image was blown away forever. I think I had a lot to do with it. When I bought my Porsche a few years later, it really shook up the caddying business!

It was a great wrench to leave Tommy after the 1979 season, but when Seve's bag became available for 1980 I went for it. I thought it was the ultimate step for any caddie. Dave Musgrove had had enough of Seve's antics, but I felt I could handle him. Mind you, Seve was a bit evil then because Dave is very thick-skinned, and he'd even got through to him. I was a very placid person, and I knew plenty about golf, so I wasn't worried about Seve's reputation.

It's very embarrassing to be shown up on the course, though, and I had a nerve-wracking start. My first tournament was in Valencia and we came to an early par-5. To carry his second shot over water he had to fly 220 metres, and Seve asked me which club. I told him it was a 3-wood but he insisted he could make it with a 1-iron. He hit his shot perfectly but it didn't carry the water by two metres or so and in it went. He turned to me in a fury and let loose like it was my fault. You just couldn't win with Seve! But you get paid by the players, so you've got to learn to take some stick. When they let off steam they go for the nearest person to them — and that's usually the caddie.

I stayed with Seve for just a year. We had four or five wins on the European Tour, so it wasn't all bad. While I'd been caddying for Seve, maybe even earlier, I'd noticed Bernhard Langer and I thought, 'this guy's going to be very good.' I next noticed him at the 1981 British Car Auctions tournament at Sunningdale, and I went up to him and asked if he wanted a regular caddie. Bernhard said he couldn't afford me, but I told him I wouldn't skin him. We had a great year and he won the European Order of Merit. We also came second in the British Open at St Georges, although realistically we weren't that close to winning it. You are always in with a chance, and when Bernhard shot a 67 in the second round I did live in hope, but it wasn't to be.

I did half of 1982 with Bernhard, but I'd not had a pay rise since I started, so I asked for one and he wouldn't agree; I decided to leave him when Greg Norman asked me to take his bag. It meant going to Australia, which didn't worry me, but I was worried if people thought I'd gone looking for Greg's bag, because he'd sacked his regular caddie, so I told him I wasn't prepared to just jump into somebody's place straight away. Greg feels money can buy everything and he wanted the top guys around him. As I had had plenty of big wins with a variety of players, he felt I was top of the caddying tree.

There was another reason why he wanted me too. During 1982 I'd caddied for a very young Gordon Brand Junior at Royal Porthcawl for the Coral Classic. Gordon won the tournament by a mile, and one of the players he beat on the way was Greg Norman, who we were drawn with in the third round. It was Gordon's first top pro tournament, and he was very raw and inexperienced. Before the tournament I told him it was no good just being a good hitter of the ball. It was a links, so I advised him to practice hard on his short game, especially his bunker play. I told him to leave things to me. 'I'll choose the club — you hit it' I said. In the newspapers reporting the tournament Greg Norman was quoted as saying that young Gordon was clearly helped by his caddie Peter Coleman. The combination proved unbeatable, said Greg, and he reckoned it was the first time he'd seen a caddie play the golfer! This was praise for me and good publicity. It made me.

As well as going out to Australia to work for Greg, I also did the 1982 Open with Bobby Clampett. We were seven shots clear with thirty holes to play — more publicity. Publicity or not, and no matter what my reputation, it just didn't work out Down Under. I didn't enjoy it, and decided to go back to Seve for 1983. We had a few wins together, and I suppose I felt I'd be staying with him but then the end of 1983 changed my mind for me.

At the end of each year a few of us used to go to Spain to work for the amateurs — Dave Musgrove and Jimmy Cousins and the like — and I was on my way back when I stopped off at the Johnnie Walker Tournament in Madrid. I had no bag because one of Seve's relations was caddying for him, his young cousin, I think. Bernhard was there with no caddie so I asked him if I could take the bag. He said that because I wasn't his regular caddie he couldn't pay me a full wage. I said I'd work for a minimal wage as long as he paid a good percentage if he won. He agreed — and then he won by four shots! I don't think he liked tipping up the money, but he asked me afterwards if I'd like to caddie for him on a regular basis again. I said yes if the wages were right and he would look after me. He agreed to everything, and ever since if I've had any problems I've just had to go to him and he's been as good as gold. Apart from the occasional visits of the yips, everything has been plain-sailing ever since.

So the second Bernhard Langer era began in 1984 and

it's still going pretty strong. We played in the majors in 1984 and it seemed to be the start of Bernhard's battle with Seve. He seemed to have a bit of a confrontation, although we always felt it was blown up. Seve beat Bernhard into second place in the Open at St Andrews, although once again we weren't in with that much of a chance. We tied with Tom Watson when he fell foul of the Road Hole. Once again I thought we could sneak it when he had a steady middle two rounds of 68–68, though. His real chance was coming the following year, his golden year.

The year 1984 finished with all the publicity about Bernhard and Seve being at each other's throats at Wentworth for the matchplay. It was really quite a laugh. Bernhard had said something about Seve in the papers before they were due to play the final. I was first into the locker-room at Wentworth and I had one of the newspapers with me that had the story in it about Bernhard having things to say about Seve. Well, Seve came in soon after me and he picked up my paper and read it. When he had beaten Bernhard in the final 2 and 1 he was asked what he thought then to Bernhard's pre-match comments, and he told the press boys he hadn't even read the story! I had a chuckle at that. It was Seve being diplomatic, for once. It was good he played things down like that because we had some fair old ding-dong battles about that time, and yet they seemed all together when it came to playing in the same Ryder Cup teams.

If Bernhard did have any hang-up about Seve's superiority he got rid of it once and for all in 1985. We started the year with a couple of good finishes on the West Coast, and then it was on to a thorough 'search' of Augusta. We play Augusta more than anybody, I think, beforehand. If there's a divot missing Bernhard knows where it's gone. He knows everything about the place.

Two shots stand out in my memory — one in the third round and one on the last day.

We'd had 72–74 for the first two rounds, not very

inspiring but we'd made the cut, and I was looking forward to a reasonable pay-day if nothing else.

Bernhard was playing really well, though, and I thought if we could just find another gear, fortunes might change for us. By well after the turn nothing earth-shaking had happened, but then on the 13th it did. I always say that for every tournament you have to have luck — good or bad luck — and you certainly need some good luck normally to win a major. On the par-5 13th (Azalea, 485 yards), Saturday, we were faced with quite a bad downhill lie for our second shot to the green, which had to be reached by crossing the brook. Augusta is renowned for its bad downhill lies, and normally you just have to take your punishment, but I had a feeling he could make it. When Bernhard said, 'I think I should just lay up because if I miss I'll be in the water,' I said, 'Let's go for it.' He didn't hit the shot very well, and the ball — at first to my horror — pitched in front of the brook, but then bounced over it and ended up on the green 10 to 12 feet from the pin. He holed the putt for an eagle! So where we could have taken six we made three. It was one of the keys to winning the tournament.

The other one came at the 17th (Nandina, 400 yards, par-4) on the final day, and I have to take some of the credit. We were hanging in there. Curtis Strange had started with an 80 on day one but fought back superbly, and he was just behind us but had hit trouble, dumping his ball into Rae's Creek. Even so, he was still breathing down our necks. After a good drive, Bernhard had the yardage left for a 7-iron, about 140–150 yards, but I could feel the adrenalin flowing; he'd been hitting the ball a long way. At the 16th he'd knocked the ball to the back of the green. So after he'd suggested the seven, I said, 'No, I think it's an eight.' He hit the shot to about six or seven feet and holed the putt for birdie! It gave him a two-shot cushion for the last, I felt. In the end, Curtis needed to birdie the last to force a playoff, but before that Bernhard could afford to make bogey five, playing safe by hitting a 1-iron off the tee. With a two-shot lead you don't take chances. We played with Seve for the last round (Strange partnered Ray Floyd in the last pairing) and it was a bonus to beat him.

That shot at the 13th on the Saturday was providence, though. It gave us the incentive to win. Two rounds of 68 to finish is evidence of that. It was a strange finish, though; no cheers much for Bernhard from the American gallery. I suppose it was because they knew Curtis had blown it and we were, after all, Europeans. They wanted an American to win. It left me feeling everything was a bit of an anticlimax, and it wasn't until I got home a few weeks later that everything sunk in. I was the first Brit to caddie a Masters winner, and Bernhard was the first European to win it. In fact only two years before it was black Augusta caddies only. I was on a bit of high because I'd been very successful, and so I didn't think winning the Masters was that important. I realised it was pretty special a bit later.

We won the Heritage Classic at Hilton Head the following week as well, so I was in the money. He'd never won a tournament in America before — and then he goes and wins two on the trot! I'd earned quite a lot of money, so I went out and bought a second-hand Porsche. I'd got ten percent of Bernhard's win and a bit from the following week's victory, so I thought I'd be a bit flash. When I went to Coombe Hill I'd been dazzled by the Porsches and Rolls Royces in the car-park and I'd vowed one day I'd have one of my own. Now I did have one. It was the highlight of my career, just as insisting on the 8-iron at the 17th was the high-spot of my caddying. I'd started off at a basic wage for my first tournament bags. Now I'd got promotion. Caddying is just like any other job; I'd gone from being office-boy to manager.

Since then I've plodded on with Bernhard. I've worked hard for him and he's had the good and bad times since the Masters win — a bit like caddying in general. People think it's an attractive life; well it is. But it's also a slog. I still don't travel Club-Class, and you have to remember a travelling

caddie has plenty of overheads — plane fares and hotels —
they're all very expensive now and you don't work for all
the fifty-two weeks of a year. There can be longish layoffs.
When Bernhard is off I find another bag. I like to keep myself busy, and it's all experience with players.

Bernhard's gone through a couple of doses of the yips
over the past few years, and his poor putting spells coincide
with his bad periods. It was only poor putting which cost
him his best chance of a British Open title. I know he'd finished second twice before, but his best chance of winning
was definitely at Sandwich in 1985 when Sandy won.
Everybody said Bernhard's second round 69 in the worst of
the weather was the best round of the week, and when he
shot a 68 in the third round which put him and David
Graham into a three-stroke lead, I thought we'd win it. He
deserved something. We really did get the worst of the
draw all week. I remember on one round having to hit two
2-woods on the 17th (425 yards, par 4) when most people
used 7- and 8-irons for their second shots. We were very
unlucky with the weather. But at the end of the day he just
didn't putt good enough to win. That was the main reason
for the 75 to finish. We ended up joint third with what
seemed a dozen other players. He still nearly forced a
playoff at the end. His chip to the 18th nearly went in —
well it actually brushed the flag. I think he might have won
the playoff. Instead he missed the one coming back and we
went back to tied third place.

There have certainly been highs and lows — like when
Bernhard five-putted the last hole in the British Open — but
I think he's appreciated me staying with him. I've had offers
from other players when he's being going through a bad
run, but they've not interested me. Then when he won the
Spanish Open in 1990 he was back on top again. He turned
round to me and said, 'Thanks for sticking with me, Pete.'
It's nice to be appreciated.

I don't work quite so hard nowadays. I take the week
more easily, rolling up on Tuesdays. Bernhard likes to do

the measuring of the course. Sometimes I do it. Sometimes I buy a yardage book. I used to get there religiously on a Monday and we'd measure the course together. I'm still very involved with club-selection and reading the greens. If I wasn't I wouldn't work. I don't want the job of just carrying a bag, I want to be involved; we're part of a team.

I know I can read greens as good as anyone. I'm not an excitable person so I can help with major decisions. Probably the caddie can make better decisions when the pressure is on the player. Most tournaments are won over the last nine holes, when the player has most pressure. That's when you've got to be the prop. In the end you want them to do what they want to do — but with your blessing, as it were, so they don't go ahead and feel they're on their own. You give the player peace of mind with the shot if you can. Sometimes the club is obvious so you can hand it over. But it's normally a case of the player saying, 'What do you think?' Then you discuss the whys and wherefores of the selection — whether it is going to fly further than normal, play short, the wind, the bounce; things like that.

For the future with Bernhard? Well, I hope he can have another year like 1987 when he won the PGA Championship returning an 18-under-par total with Wentworth playing its full length, and the Irish Open at Portmarnock 19-under-par. They could play a tournament at Portmarnock every week of the year and not get to 19-under. But that's how it is with Bernhard. You get those sort of weeks. Another week and he's gone from Jeckyll back to Hyde, normally when his putting's gone off again. Putting's always been the key to whether Bernhard's on form. He's changed his putting action so many times it makes me dizzy thinking about it. The only way I've been able to help is to try to give him confidence on the green. The yips are a state of mind. Your hands try to do what your brain is telling them but they can't. The way Bernhard putts now, holding the crook of his elbow, takes his hands right out of it. He putts with his shoulder. All you can do is instil confidence for his method of the moment. There's no telling how long it will last! Sometimes I've felt like weeping for him. People have said when he was going through one of his bad patches, 'Why don't you get out. He's costing you money.' The money doesn't interest me. He's a great bloke.

Bernhard always gives 100 percent. When he's paid appearance money he earns it. Some players don't want to respond when they have started badly. That's not the case with Bernhard. Take St Mellion in the 1990 Benson and Hedges International. At the first hole he had a quadruple-bogey eight after a cruel lie; then a bogey at the next hole. After two holes he's five-over-par. He just got his head down, got back into it and went on to the leaderboard. It's good to know you're out there with a guy who's trying 100 percent. I have great respect for him. It's been a big regret that we've never won an Open, but it may still be on the cards. There can be no atmosphere and buzz like walking down the 18th of an Open Championship — the crescendo of noise makes it like a stadium. I'd like us to get that reception. It would be nice to walk down the last with a two-shot lead.'

# Fanny Sunesson

*Caddying has traditionally been a male bastion, and the females in the bag-carrying ranks of the world's top men professionals are few and far between. But 1989 saw the bastion breached as a young Swedish girl, who had been working on the European Tour for only two years or so, made her presence felt in the caddying ranks. She was to go on to be the first European lady caddie to carry in the Ryder Cup — and then, re-markably, to add a major honour to her short career honours. That young Swede is Fanny Sunesson. She has not yet put herself among the ranks of the caddies who can tell 'how we won the Open', but that will not be too long coming, surely?*

*When Nick Faldo decided to change his caddie to start the 1990 sea-son there were a few heads nodded; it seemed almost as big a decision as the one he made to change his swing. In the end the swing-change proved far more traumatic than the caddie-change, as Faldo became only the second player in Masters history to attain back-to-back victories at Augusta.*

*Faldo achieved his second Masters success in 1990 with 22-year-old Fanny from Gothenburg, having taken her on to care for his bag in preference to his caddie of long standing, Andy Prodger from England. Faldo felt he and Prodger were 'no longer communicating', and so forced the parting of their ways. Nick had won a string of titles either side of the Atlantic with Prodger, including two majors, the 1987 British Open and the US Masters of 1989.*

*Faldo spent two years re-shaping his swing well enough to win the 1987 Open at Muirfield, but would changing the winning partnership of Faldo/Prodger to Faldo/Sunesson also work out? That question was answered in the cauldron of one of the most thrilling US Masters ever seen at Augusta. Fanny came through with flying colours, made herself into a celebrity in her own right, and in a short time has become a golfing personality, much sought after by the media especially.*

*Fanny started her caddying career having to room with the male caddies on tour, and generally has had to take the rough with the smooth on the road, just like anybody.*

@ @ @

'The men were great when I first started. Everyone was very helpful and caring. I used to room with them, but there was no funny business. We all had our job to do. I switched to staying with a girl-friend while on tour, but now I stay in hotels on my own.'

@ @ @

*Caddies' Association chairman Martin Rowley remembers, 'No one looked upon her as a woman, although she definitely is! She was just another caddie on the road. We're all rake-rats together'.*

*Becoming a rake-rat started for Fanny at around seven years of age, when she first started playing golf with her parents. She played a lot of golf as a youngster, and eventually got down to the five handicap she holds currently. Playing to such a standard — in a rare appearance on*

*the course playing in 1989 she shot consecutive rounds of 76 — has ena-
bled her to understand all the rudiments of the golf swing, a great help
when Faldo wanted her to understand his swing and the teaching of his
coach David Leadbetter before they tackled the 1990 US Masters.*

*Just knowing golf and being a proficient player was not enough for
Fanny, though. She wanted to be 'inside the ropes' when the bell went for
the top tournaments, not outside spectating. After watching the 1985
Scandinavian Open she determined that the following year she would try
for a bag at the same event. Fanny rolled up to the 1986 Scandinavian
with one thought: to caddie in the tournament. One by one, the players
who were not already fixed up with caddies selected their partners.
Fanny was beginning to think she was going to miss out when 1984
Tournament Players Champion Jamie Gonzalez from Brazil took her on.
She was the penultimate caddie to be hired for the tournament! Gonzalez
and Fanny hit it off, and the Brazilian asked her to caddie for him at the
following week's tournament, also in Sweden, the PLM Open.*

*Fanny had made it. She decided there was a future for her alongside
the men on the European Tour. It meant next having to take a bus across
Europe for the following month's tour events, but she landed the bags of
English players Chris Moody and Mark Wiltshire, two of Europe's well-
known journeymen with just the sort of experience she needed. News of
her expertise spread, and another stalwart of the tour, another Englishman too, Andrew Murray, asked Fanny to take his bag when the 1987
season started. Murray was steady but too staid for Fanny, and she had
now raised her game on the ambitions front. She dearly wanted to carry a
bag for the Ryder Cup.*

*Manuel Pinero's caddie Jimmy Cousins then gave her what she feels
was her biggest break — fixing her up with Spaniard Jose Rivero's bag.
Rivero had already featured in the Ryder Cup, and it looked as though he
was in with a good chance of making the 1987 team for Muirfield Village.
But it was 'no-way, Jose', and Rivero missed out on a Ryder Cup place.
So Fanny felt it was time to move on. This meant the bags of Roger Chap-
man from England, a great tour player but seemingly destined to be
Europe's 'nearly' man, and her Swedish compatriot Anders Forsbrand,
who appeared to have a very bright future before him. They all added to
Fanny's player experience, as she marched the fairways in her distinctive
style in 1988.*

*It was on to 1989 and another Ryder Cup year. Fanny decided to
make her bid again for a player who might give her that sought-after
Ryder Cup bag — this time at The Belfry in England. She asked York-*

*shireman Howard Clark if she could carry his bag in 1989 and he agreed.*
*It was a great bonus that Clark should clinch his Ryder Cup place within*
*a week of playing in her native Sweden.*

*The Belfry of September 1989 fulfilled Fanny's Ryder Cup dream*
*and so what next? The British Open? The US Masters? When Nick*
*Faldo, whose coach David Leadbetter had also re-vamped Clark's swing*
*so sucessfully, asked her to take over from Andy Prodger, she jumped at*
*the chance of working alongside arguably the world's top golfer of the*
*moment. Ironically, Fanny is not far off the same height as Prodger. She*
*is about 5 ft 6 ins to the top of her shock of brown/blonde ponytail.*
*Neither she nor Andy look big enough to haul Faldo's tournament bag to*
*major success, but without any special kinetic training, Fanny seems to*
*manage it with ease. The only time it starts to get really heavy, she main-*
*tains, is when Faldo is not playing well. When he is on song, she hardly*
*knows it is there! Ever the perfectionist, Faldo took Fanny to see his coach*
*David Leadbetter and before the Masters bid they all got their heads*
*together to discuss the technicalities and techniques required of Faldo's*
*swing and method at Augusta.*

Being a five-handicapper I understand the swing, and
particularly Nick's swing, and the three of us got together before practice to talk over a few things. It put me at
ease.

I don't read the lines on the greens for Nick. He does
that himself. But we do discuss clubs and decide on club
selection. That proved very important on the last day. The
first three rounds were fairly ordinary, so much so that I
can't remember them without referring to notes. All I remember is that we had two bad clubs on the first day. We
bogeyed the first and the third because we got the wind
wrong. On the last day I have a good memory to keep. As I
say, we discuss club selection. He says a club and I have to
say what I think. Sometimes we change it. I changed him on
the fourth hole (Palm, 220 yards, par-3). He said 3-iron and I
said 4-iron. He hit the 4-iron perfectly and that gave me
great satisfaction. On the last day, I thought Nick would

have to play really well, which he did, and Ray Floyd would have to make a mistake, which he did. I was never nervous on the course but when we had finished the round I was shaking. Ray was still out on the course and I was so nervous I could nearly not stand up. When I knew there was a playoff, though, my nerves went as soon as I went back out on to the course. I got on with the job again. When Nick had won he gave me some of the praise. That was nice, but I didn't hit the shots. I just tried to help. We are a team, it's true, but a caddie can only do so much. A player can be without a caddie but a caddie can't be without a player!

🍺 🍺 🍺

*Obviously teamwork is the key to a bright future. Just as we prepared to go to press, the Nick Faldo–Fanny Sunesson combination came up trumps at the 119th British Open Championship at St. Andrews. The bubbly Swedish caddie played a great part in Faldo's second major win of the year, which came only months after he retained his title in the US Masters, and only weeks after he finished joint third in the US Open. Although in these events Fanny had not been greatly involved in reading the lines on the greens for Faldo, who felt that success depended on his 'feel', this changed the week before the British Open. While playing in the Scottish Open at Gleneagles during the build-up to St. Andrews, Faldo confessed, Fanny had 'unlocked some of the putting mysteries' that had been confounding him.*

*In Fanny Sunesson's first year with Nick Faldo their performance looks set to out-achieve that of any other player–caddie partnership in a single year in major championship golf.*

# INDEX

Page numbers in **bold** indicate photographs.

# INDEX

# INDEX

# ACKNOWLEDGEMENTS

My grateful thanks to the men with bags under their eyes, and especially to Willie Aitchison who did the sergeant-major bit. Thanks also to George Reid at the Dunvegan Hotel — yet another caddie, incidentally — for his help. By no means least, thanks to 'Dusty' for making me believe in myself.

## Picture Credits

Peter Dazeley: pages 49 (top), 112
Phil Sheldon: pages 49 (bottom), 50, 55 (top), 57, 105, 107, 108, 110, 111
Yours in Sport: pages 51, 55 (bottom), 106
Gerry Cranham: pages 52, 53, 54, 109